50 YEARS
OF STAGE AND SCREEN

50 YEARS STAGE AND SCREEN

LEEDS THEATRES AND CINEMAS REMEMBERED

by Arthur Riley

Wharncliffe Publishing

First Published in 1999 by
Wharncliffe Publishing
an imprint of
Pen and Sword Books Limited,
47 Church Street, Barnsley,
South Yorkshire. S70 2AS

Copyright © Wharncliffe Publishing 1999

*For up-to-date information on other titles produced under the
Wharncliffe imprint, please telephone or write to:*

> Wharncliffe Publishing
> FREEPOST
> 47 Church Street
> Barnsley
> South Yorkshire S70 2BR
> Telephone (24 hours): 01226 - 734555

ISBN: 1-871647-69-X

A CIP catalogue record of this book is available from the
British Library

Cover illustration: From the Arthur Riley collection

Printed in Great Britain by
Redwood Books, Trowbridge, Wiltshire

CONTENTS

In memory of my dear wife, Chico who supported me in all my endeavours and gave this story its original working title of 'Cue One'.

I would like to thank all my friends and colleagues, who suggested that I put my reminiscences into book form, and who on so many occasions reminded me of events or verified details.

A special thanks must go to Shirley Haines, who produced the first typed manuscript. Finally, with many thanks to Lynne Stevenson Tate, for her patient and thorough editorial work, without which this story would not have been published.

*Cue 1–*BEGINNINGS

I WAS BORN ON 5 AUGUST 1921 in the delightful village of Dacre, near Penrith in Cumberland, now known as Cumbria. Dacre is one mile from Ullswater. My parents were Albert and Martha Amelia Riley, née Franks, but my father nicknamed her 'Patty'. He was employed as a chauffeur for two sisters, the Misses Brown of Dacre Lodge Mansion who were 'lady farmers'. We lived in a cottage near to the mansion, which had the name of Dacre Lodge Cottage and was built in 1774 by James Hodgson.

Besides my parents, my family consisted eventually of Albert, Fred, Ellen, Thomas Eric, a sister who passed away at the age of two and a half months, Lila and myself, Arthur Havelock Riley. My father had been a soldier in the First World War with the Leeds Rifles. He was wounded and carried a piece of shrapnel lodged in his body for the rest of his life. As an old soldier he wanted one of his sons to carry the name of a famous soldier from history.

General Sir Henry Havelock served in India from 1823. During the Indian Mutiny in 1857/58 he organized a force of 1000 Highlanders and others at Allahabad and from there he proceeded to relieve Cawnpore and Lucknow. Due to sickness amongst his small army Havelock had to retire to Cawnpore. Reinforcements arrived in the September under General Outram. Havelock and Outram joined forces and the combined force fought their way to Lucknow and occupied the residency there, but were trapped and besieged until November when Sir Colin Campbell arrived with reinforcements. On the 22 November, a week after the relief, Havelock by now a

Albert Riley with the Lagonda at Newton Kyme Hall, near Tadcaster, c1927.

Newton Kyme Hall, near Tadcaster in 1999.

KCB, died of dysentery. His widow received the rank of a baronet's widow and a pension of £1,000. The baronetcy was conferred on his son, later Sir Henry Havelock Allen VC. The honour of carrying the name from military history fell to me, which is how I came to have the middle name of Havelock.

When I was about six years old father became chauffeur to Lord and Lady Briggs-Robinson at Newton Kyme Hall near Tadcaster, and mother was cook-general with eight staff under her. It was all very much like the 1970s series *Upstairs Downstairs*. We lived in a converted barn cottage in the village and I sang in the local church choir. For these services I received 1/- and a loaf of bread. I was sent from here to audition at the Bluecoates School that was attached to York Minster, where choir boys were trained and although I passed the audition, circumstances prevented me from taking up the opportunity.

*Cue 2–*CINEMA LIFE

IN 1935, AT THE AGE OF FOURTEEN I left Allerton High School, Bradford. The next step in my life was work, which meant a visit to the Labour Exchange where I was given a green card to go along to the *Theatre Royal*, Manningham Lane, Bradford.

On my arrival I was shown into the manager's office. The position on offer was as rewind boy in the projection room. The manager took me down a flight of steps and we approached a large metal door which he opened. The room beyond was in darkness except for a couple of bright lights and the noise of a projector screening a sound film. A voice said 'Stand by for Cue One' and another said 'Motor' and within seconds the shout of 'Over' followed. Then all the lights in the room were switched on to reveal the projection suite. This was to be the beginning of my life in Cinema.

***Theatre Royal*, Bradford c1950.**

The words 'Cue One' are used when a dot appears on the right hand side of the screen; this indicates that the reel of film is eleven feet from the end. This alerts the projectionist on the second projector to start the change over. We shouted 'Over' on the last dot. On this last dot the projectionist switched the sound over from the outgoing reel to reel two. The outgoing shot of film is cut off at the same time as the sound. This was where my job as rewind boy came in.

I was introduced to the chief projectionist, Reg Dalby and the second projectionist, John Sanderson. Mr Dalby interviewed me and showed me round. From one of the rooms came a whining noise, this was the generating room where generators supplied DC current for the arc lamps. The generator was a BTH and a later model was known as the Ruston Hornsby.

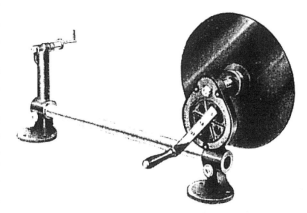

During the interview the importance of the rewind boy's job was stressed. As each reel of film came off the projector it was checked to ensure that it would run through the next projector without breaking. After removing the outgoing film from the bottom spool box on the projector it then had to be taken to the rewind room which was fifteen feet long and six feet wide with good clear lighting. In here were two metal topped benches, one on each side. The right hand end of the bench was fitted with a rewind arm which had an empty metal spool on it. The spool of film to be rewound was placed on a spindle at the left hand end. The film travelled through the projectors at ninety feet a

Kaylee Rewinder used for rewinding film whilst checking for breakages, cut sprocket holes and dry joints.

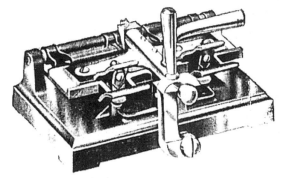

A Rigby Joining Press: as used by the rewind boy when repairing damaged film.

Typical projectors and arc lamp bulbs (opposite) used in cinemas during the 1930s and 1940s. *Author's collection*

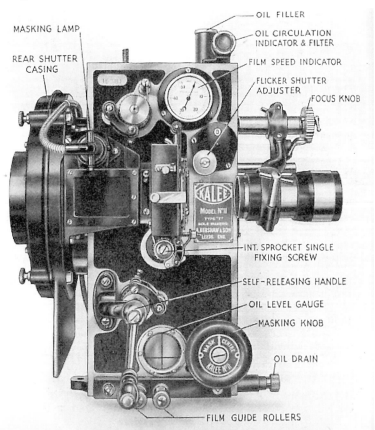

minute or twenty-four frames a second. Some of the spools held 1,700 to 2,000 feet of film and it had to be rewound by hand. The left hand held the film lightly to maintain the necessary tension as it was wound onto the empty spool. Whilst winding, the rewind boy had to check for damage to the film. Damaged sprocket holes and dry joints had to be repaired on a splicing and editing machine. Joints were stuck with film amelacetone, acetic acid and acetone which when mixed together made a cement. Once the reel had been checked it was placed in a film can which had the title and number of the reel on a card. For example, cartoon, travel or news films were all on single spools. A main feature film of ten reels would be marked 'Feat 1.2-3.4-5.6-7.8-9.10. All were on single reels but on making up a programme they were linked as indicated on a card. Some feature films, such as *Marie Antoinette* could have as many as fourteen reels. The films of that time included a chemical during the manufacturing process called nitrate, which was highly flammable and hence rather dangerous. If the film caught fire it burned fiercely and was hard to put out, so all the doors, the rewind bench, film bin and spools, were metal covered to prevent the spread of fire. If the worst happened there were sand buckets in every room and over each projector was an asbestos sheet or blanket which would drop down and envelop a burning projector at the pull of a release cord. All the rooms had to be kept spotlessly clean to further reduce fire risk.

The technical bible used by cinema managers and which now changes hands for £100 per copy. *Author's collection*

Diesel powered generators were the usual standby power system during the 1930s and 1940s. *Author's collection*

On accepting the position at the *Theatre Royal*, I was informed that there was a ban on smoking and drinking by cinema personnel in the areas where film was handled. Due to volatility of the nitrate film the danger of fire from this film was very real.

The *Theatre Royal* in previous years had been an outstanding repertory theatre; the finest actor who made his final appearance there in October 1905, was the great Sir Henry Irving. Sir Henry played a succession of major roles during his last week in Bradford. On 9 October he played Shylock in *The Merchant of Venice*, on 10 October the title role in Tennyson's *Becket*, while on the 11 October it was *Louis XI*. The play on 12 October was *The Bells*. This was the same play he and Ellen Terry had given as a command performance for Queen Victoria at Sandringham in 1898. On 13 October he again took the part of Becket. He died later the same evening, at his hotel.

A plaque which paid homage to him was installed in the foyer of the *Theatre Royal*. This was later removed and taken to the *Midland*

Hotel in Bradford where it was attached to the outside wall. Subsequently two telephone boxes were built in front of the plaque. Many years later it was found to have disappeared.

The first film that I rewound and checked was *Limelight*; not the Chaplin one but a circus one starring Tulio Carmeneta, John Loder and Anna Neagle. Arthur Tracy sang a song in it called *The Whistling Waltz*. At my then tender age of fourteen how could I know that Anna Neagle and Arthur Tracy (the Street Singer) were to play a part in my life in years to come.

A Ruston horizontal diesel engine which was used to drive cinema generators in the 1930s and 1940s. *Courtesy of Ray Hooley collection*

*Cue 3–*Bigger Things on Screen

MY FAMILY MOVED TO LEEDS in 1936 when I was fifteen and a half years old, and I obtained work at what was then the finest cinema in Leeds, the *Paramount* theatre, which had 2590 seats. What an experience for me! Two big films, an organ recital and a stage show in between the big films, all for the seat price of 7d. Ice-cream and sweets of your choice were available at Meeson's sweet shop just outside the main door. Eventually the sweets, popcorn, ice-creams and such were introduced for sale inside the theatre.

In the early years of the cinema the American moguls of the film industry had a saying, 'Give 'em a load of baloney and boy they'll (the patrons) come a-running'. So there were big movies and even bigger stars. The first major film I wound and checked at the

Gracie Fields performed in stage shows at the Paramount c1962.

Paramount, was *The Westerner* which starred Gary Cooper. In this film there is a long shot of an anonymous Indian brave on his horse. That was the first sighting on film of Anthony Quinn, who was married at that time to the daughter of Cecil B De Mille, who made the film. There was also lots of baloney, with films like *The Beast from 20,000 Fathoms.*

The stage shows included many later famous names. The Mills Brothers first appearance in England was at the *Paramount*; Gracie Fields, who corresponded with me for forty-four years up to her death; Arthur Tracy (the Street Singer): Elizabeth Welch, who also wrote to me often; Paul Robeson, Adelaide Hall, Jack Payne and his band, Jack Hylton, Teddy Joyce and his Sweethearts, Oliver Wakefield, Gene Autry (I never thought I would meet my favourite cowboy in the flesh!), Tom Mix and many, many more. It was my job to collect from the performers on a Monday the 'colours' for the spotlight when they were on stage. These were made up from sheets of coloured gelatine. I worked the 'spots' from the projection room. It was essential to many of the performers to have the right background colour at the right point in the act.

When the stage shows were on I was put on the microphone control board, which was at the right hand side of the back circle. My job was to adjust the microphone settings so that there was no feed back or screeching noises when the artistes were on stage.

Among the organists who appeared were Jack Lawton, Cecil Chadwick and Leeds' own Henry Croudson. They put on different programmes but, without exception, when the organist played a piece entitled *Trees*, a green design slide was projected onto the screen, then a plain blue slide followed by a third slide with the words to *Trees* on and the patrons sang along. The slide machine was called a Brenograph. This piece of equipment was first introduced as the Ross Sceneograph and consisted of slides and effects. In the Brenograph a lens turret is provided for each of the three lanterns and the light is reflected by adjustable mirrors to any part of the screen or stage. It is best if one imagines three of the modern 35mm colour slide projectors stacked one on top of the other, all projecting a different image which combined together to make one composite whole. The first lantern carried a slide with the design; the second lantern was equipped with a colour wheel which projected the colour onto the screen; and the third contained the words to a popular song that the organist was playing which enabled the patrons to sing along. Slides were also used to advertise forthcoming film and local businesses. These slides consisted of two pieces of glass; the first was

A typical projection room layout. Although this is at the *Warner Theatre* in London, the *Paramount* layout was identical. At the far end is the spotlight used for the organ and stage shows. Two more spots would be at the right hand side of the photograph, just out of sight.

coloured and the second had the advert on. These were then sandwiched together with heat resistant tape. One person operated the Brenograph whilst another shone the spotlight on the organist.

The organ was housed below the stage, and at a given signal from the organist it would rise up into view at the side of the stage. At the end of the organ show there was another signal and the organ sank out of sight and after a second or two the curtains opened with the footlights on and the film began. When a stage show was presented the curtains were closed and the screen was raised electrically, out of sight, at the push of a button. A band could be accommodated on stage or in the band pit, which, like the organ, could be raised and lowered electronically.

If a patron was hard of hearing, certain seats in the theatre were fitted with a socket, and the usher provided a pair of headphones which, when plugged into the socket made the soundtrack clear for them to enjoy. In some cases these headphones were fed not directly from the main amplifier system but from a separate amplifier connected to a microphone suitably placed near the main speakers. Each pair of headphones was provided with its own volume control, and sometimes a tone control, since many deaf people have difficulty in hearing the upper frequencies which give speech its intelligibility. In one system, instead of headphones needing to be plugged in, a miniature amplifier was provided with each pair, energised by induction from a copper network placed underneath the carpet, and fed from the speaker circuits. The copper network acted as an aerial. This system is still used today and is called an induction loop system.

Part of my duties as rewind boy was to collect the film in single reels from the Film Transport Services situated in Clarence Road. These reels were in turn housed in a large metal box. If I was lucky I would be able to catch a tram back to the *Paramount*. However because of the nitrate film only one film at a time was allowed to be carried on the tram as the box, of necessity, would be standing only a short distance away from the transformer on the vehicle. It was thought that the field generated by the transformer could cause the nitrate to ignite. At the *Paramount* the 'Staff Only' entrance was next to Meeson's sweet shop and I had to go up a metal spiral staircase which passed the side door of the kitchen for the cafe.

On one occasion I had been to collect *Sixty Glorious Years*, which was to be premiered that night. As I was going up this staircase with the heavy metal box on my shoulder, I stepped on a partly cooked piece of bacon which had been dropped on the staircase near the kitchen door. I slipped on it and fell backwards. A long piece of metal on the lid of the film box pierced my neck; fortunately as staff were continually coming and going on the staircase I was soon found and taken to the old dispensary on North Street, just past the *Tower Cinema*. Needless to say Chef was seen by the manager! I was back at the *Paramount* within two hours with my neck bandaged. As I loved my job I continued with making up and rewinding the film. It was to be premiered that night with Anna Neagle appearing in person.

At the premiere all those staff who were free at the time were invited to meet the stars. I took my turn in the line-up still heavily bandaged. When Anna Neagle got to me she asked what had happened. I recounted the story to her.

She laughed, but then in a more serious mood said, 'You must write to me informing me of how you progress,' and a lady with her handed me a card with Miss Neagle's address. Throughout the years until Anna Neagle's death in 1986 we corresponded regularly.

As I mentioned earlier it was my job each Monday to collect 'colour sheets' from the stage artistes who were appearing in person between the films. On one occasion the delightful piano duo Rawicz and Landauer were appearing, and when I went to collect the colour

Rawicz and Landauer.

Elizabeth Welch.

sheet they asked me in broken English, 'Do you night club in the city?'.

I told them that as I was under age I did not smoke or drink; however I informed my chief projectionist of their request and he took them to the *101* in New York Street. For his kindness the famous duo bought him a gift of a gold cigarette case, which was quite something in those days. On the final night of their visit I took the colour sheets back to them and requested a signed photograph.

They were signing this and one of them said, 'Vot is your name?', so I replied, 'Arthur'.

He replied, 'I don't like Arthur - I put George instead.'

Miss Elizabeth Welch was a guest on one of our Sunday concerts. She was an exciting singer of jazz versions of beloved standards which she embellished with wonderful facial expressions. She was the beautiful star of *Tuppence Coloured* and she was a friend of, and had acted with, Mr Paul Robeson. During the evening of her show the weather was terrible. After the concert I had to check back stage, around the electrics and so on, and Miss Welch was still in the stage door area where the telephone was, trying,without success, to get a taxi to take her to the *Queen's Hotel*. Outside the rain was getting worse but by now annoyed, she said that if she knew the way to the *Queen's Hotel*, she would walk. I immediately offered to escort her there, so, with my raincoat over both our shoulders I walked her to the hotel. She made a note of my home address and sent me a signed photo, and from then on corresponded with me each year when she took a holiday in London. In 1998 at the age of eighty-nine she sold her London home and returned to live in Harlem.

Cue 4–ARTHUR MOBILE

ON THE FOURTH OF NOVEMBER 1939 I married Minnie Cork, who I had nicknamed 'Chico' because of her liking for coffee. This was also the year I volunteered for the RAF, but failed my medical which was held at Hoover House behind Vicar Lane in Leeds. I was categorised Grade 4. This meant I was unfit for active service, due to damaged eardrums from an accident years before.

In 1940, after four years at the *Paramount*, I was offered the second projectionist position at the *Tatler* on Boar Lane. Shortly afterwards the manager, Mr C Shaverin, thought that I would be a suitable replacement for the chief projectionist, a Mr Burgess, who was leaving. Mr Burgess' son Jackie, was also on the staff in

Arthur and Minnie, 'Chico', on their tenth wedding anniversary.

The Tatler, Boar Lane.

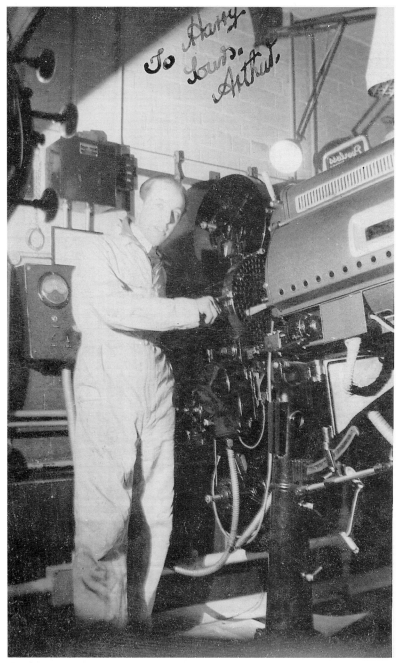

Arthur in the projection room of *The Tatler* c1941.

Arthur with Alan Hullah on a roof overlooking Mill Hill Chapel in City Square.

the projection room as rewind boy and the third projectionist was Bernard Noble. With my promotion, all the staff were promoted up, which then meant that we required a new rewind boy. This position went to a young man called Alan Hullah, who was not only excellent at his job, but he became a close friend of our family; when our son Jeffrey was born my wife suggested that his middle name should be Alan. Coincidentally this meant that Jeffrey's initials, JAR also represented one J Arthur Rank.

The *Tatler* cinema screened 'repertory' films such as *Rose Marie* and *The Firefly*. In 1940-41 we were to screen for four weeks *Pastor Hall* based on the life of a German priest, Pastor Martin Niemoller. The title role was played by Wilfred Lawson, and portraying a German camp officer was Bernard Miles. This actor fascinated me, although he only had a small part with not much dialogue. In November, during the second week of screening this film, the play *Thunder Rock* was playing at the *Grand Theatre* in Leeds with a small part in it played by the same Bernard Miles. I wrote to him and mentioned that we were screening *Pastor Hall* and asked for a signed photograph. Two days later our doorman at the *Tatler*, Joe Robinson, came up to the projection room remarking, 'Oh, Mr Riley, the chap who is the German Officer in the film is in the foyer wanting to see you.' I did wonder if the staff were pulling my leg; however I went down to the foyer and Bernard Miles introduced himself and his co-star in *Thunder Rock*, the Sudeten/German star Frederick Valk. Bernard handed me signed photographs of himself and souvenirs. Then he remarked, 'Arthur, a relation of mine from Australia is with me. He has never seen how films are screened. Would you show him please?' How could I refuse a request like that? I was proud that I knew my job. Later I asked Bernard if the cinema manager could have a press interview for publicity purposes and he agreed and the *Yorkshire Evening Post* came round and gave the front page to Bernard and the *Tatler*. As chief projectionist this was my first taste of arranging publicity stunts. Bernard and I remained friends from that time on, until his death.

During the war the *Tatler* showed many Ministry of Information films and one day in 1943 Mr Madison, who was the head of this

Bernard Miles in his role for the film *Pastor Hall*, signed and dated November 1940

Fredrick Valk.

Arthur's mobile cinema (MOI) c1941. Notice that the audience face the screen mounted in the rear of the van on which the film is back projected. Notice too the speakers mounted on the roof.

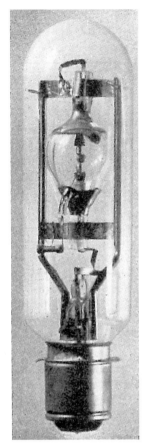

Type of lamp used in 16mm projectors.

service paid us a visit. I still wished to do something for the war effort and I asked him how one applied to join the Ministry of Information (MOI) mobile cinema unit which showed 16mm information films throughout England to the troops, Land Army, munitions workers, in fact anywhere such informational films needed to be seen. He told me and, along with many other applicants, I qualified on the technical test and was taken on. Our training took place at Blackheath Film Studios where our chief instructor was a technician called Mr S Procopeadous. Mr Procopeadous was a Greek and had invented a curved 'gate' on the GBII/56 16mm sound projector which we used. He put us through a thorough training programme but as we were all qualified projectionists in civilian life, we did not find the operation and maintenance of the 16mm sound projector hard to follow. Whilst we were in London we were also taught to drive, as we would be required to travel widely once we started work.

The 16mm projector along with a transformer were fitted into a small cubicle at the rear of the driving seat in a large Bedford van. The film was beamed onto the back of a large screen which was positioned only two feet away from the projector. This was called rear projection as the audience stood or sat around the back of the van which was painted all in black to give better clarity to the projected image. Sound was relayed through two large speakers on the roof of the van. These were detachable, which enabled me to place them in the rear of the van after each show.

There were two methods by which we powered the projector. When a show was given in a barracks, school, village hall, government offices and the like, then the ordinary mains supply was used. The projector along with a mobile screen mounted on a tripod which was carried as part of our standard equipment, was set up in the indoor area. We had various lenses which enabled us to line up the picture at whatever distance we were away from the screen. The two speakers also had stands. The bulb used to illuminate the screen and picture was about six inches tall and two inches in circumference.

When we were at a venue where no mains electricity was available we used a small JAP petrol generator, which was also carried as standard issue. This generator provided the necessary power to run the projector, lamp and sound equipment. The JAP was a two stroke engine and had to be hand cranked to start it just like the early motor cars. This cranking had to be carried out correctly as incorrect methods had resulted in broken wrists for some projectionists. The projectors were very portable and my love for this type of equipment created my own hobby on my return to 'civvy street'. I designed and built my own home cinemas in all the houses we lived in; in attic, spare bedroom and even a large cellar.

The Ministry of Information tried to base all its projectionists as near as possible to their own home areas, but while I was awaiting my posting I worked in London. This was the most exciting area to be in. Whilst I was there, the Ministry of Food held an exhibition in the headquarters of one of the railway companies, and Mrs Eleanor Roosevelt, the wife of President Roosevelt, came along to open the it and after the show asked me questions about my work and my life in general. Another show was at the Yugoslavian Embassy for ex-King Peter who was in exile in this country. His aide-de-camp had got the films that his Highness had requested to see. The feature was entitled *A Night in Belgrade*, and in my view could only be graded as 'X' certificate. Some of the scenes were rather near the bone, but as the dialogue was in Serbo-Croatian I could make neither head nor tail of the storyline. The ex-king and his guest were satisfied though, and he thanked me through his interpreter.

The main office of the Ministry of Information in Yorkshire was at 7 Wetherby Road, Leeds. However, I was to be based at Barnsley, working in the Hull, Penistone, Sheffield, Withernsea, Hornsea and Doncaster areas. I remember visiting the British Rope Works in Doncaster and the nearby ICI factory, showing all the propaganda films allotted by the Ministry of Information. They had titles such as *Fighter Pilot*, *Kill or be Killed*, *Foam Fighting* and the like. The workers attended when they were able and as a full twenty-four hour shift system was in operation, it meant that I had to be in attendance at all hours, even between 1.00am and 3.00am. We showed films in factories, at Land Army hostels, army barracks, RAF and Navy stations, wherever and whenever necessary. We often slept in barrack rooms and drank seemingly endless mugs of cocoa which would allegedly help us go to sleep. Recently my attention was drawn to a news report from the remote Highlands of Scotland. There a 50 foot mobile cinema, costing £660,000, is now operating. It transforms into a 110 seater cinema and is called the Screen Machine. Although the Highlands are home to 310,000 people, only six of the many scattered communities have permanent cinemas. The first use of this cinema was in the Highland village of Newtonmore.

Cue Five–PROMOTION CALLS ME

AFTER THE WAR MY POSITION at the *Tatler* was still there for me and in due course I became engineer with the parent company which operated *News Theatre*, and the *Tatler* cinemas. All went well until a new manager came to the *News Theatre*, named Stefan Soboki. Mr Soboki was a Polish gentleman who knew nothing whatever about the cinema business, but was a friend of the owner Mr Fennel, who was based in Manchester.

Mr Soboki was under the impression that the *Tatler*, my base, received more attention than his *News Theatre*, and when breakdowns occurred, such as when the films ran off, the lighting was bad and so on, he was heard to remark that his operators 'were bloody'. Two weeks after his first utterance of this remark, a sheet of paper went on the notice board in the *News Theatre* projection room entitled *How to Show films*. Soboki it seemed, had copied this out of a film book.

I pulled this sheet down and dashed into his office and explained that the notice was an insult to my staff and my final remark was,

The *Odeon*, Manchester Road, Bradford.

Queue for Stromboli outside the *Empire Cinema*, Morley Street, Bradford.

'The trouble with you bloody foreigners is, you come into this trade without knowing nothing about it.' The owner, Mr Fennel was called in to deal with this matter and he told me if I was willing to apologise to Mr Soboki I could stay with the company. I refused, and resigned. Shortly after I mentioned this incident in a letter to Bernard Miles. Back came a reply with the message, 'Get yourself along to the Odeon, Bradford. A position is open for you as assistant manager.'

I went to Bradford and met with Mr Mervyn Morse, who was to become my manager at the *Odeon*. The *Odeon* cinema on Manchester Road, Bradford, was new and doing good business. Training was both strict and comprehensive; one month I was on duty with the head doorman working on how to get the queues in; one month on how to usher patrons to their seats; one month with the cleaners, and one month in the projection room. After only one week the chief projectionist remarked that, considering my experience, he saw no need for me to be with him any longer. Sometime later while waiting for a hair cut in the gents hairdressing department of Lewis' in Leeds, who should be waiting beside me on the long seat but Mr Soboki. 'Good Morning Mr Soboki' I said and he replied, 'Mr Riley, they call me Mr Smith now. I changed my name by deed poll. I have left the News Theatre and I'm now into jewellery!'

As assistant manager one of my first jobs each morning was the banking of the the previous day's takings. The manager and I simply walked to and from the bank around 9.30am each day! Later there were the advertising schedules to prepare for forthcoming films. These were prepared up to a month ahead for the *Yorkshire Evening Post* and the Bradford *Telegraph & Argus*, and gave a synopsis of the story lines of the films which were sent out from the *Odeon* headquarters.

Another of my jobs was publicity in and around the premises. In the upstairs foyer where there were seats for the patrons waiting to go into the circle there was an imitation palm tree, and by the rear wall was a large wooden *Odeon* on which were squares and slots where I would put in still photographs of films we were due to screen. One afternoon, on my manager's day off, I was busy putting in the new stills for the display. The weather outside was shocking, and patrons were coming up to the circle foyer wet through, shaking raincoats and umbrellas everywhere. As I turned round I saw among the patrons two of J Arthur Rank's top stars, Googie Withers and John McCullum; they were not married at that time. I moved forward to Miss Withers, introducing myself and at the same time helping her to remove her wet outdoor clothing, a red cape with a hood. At this time

Miss Withers and Mr McCullum were in the middle of shooting a light romantic comedy drama called *A Boy, a Girl and a Bike*, about a Yorkshire cycling club. The story was set around Huddersfield. The director, Ralph Smart introduced me to John McCullum and the rest of the cast and crew. Because of the bad weather they had called a halt to filming and decided to come to the cinema. They had chosen this one because Miss Withers was a great fan of Charles Laughton who was the star of *The Big Clock*. which we were screening at the time.

I mustered the staff to organise the drying off of wet clothes and before Miss Withers went in to see the film I asked her if I could call the local press; she agreed but stipulated that there was to be only one flash photograph of her watching the film. These arrangements were completed and I escorted the party to the front seats in the circle. The press came and took only one flash photograph as agreed. This chance for further 'promotions' went to my head a little and I pondered my next move. Tea for the entire party when they had seen the film?. We had no cafe, but across the main road facing the cinema was a delightful cafe, with waitresses and so on; so, with the co-operation of the manager of the cafe a wonderful meal was brought across into our upstairs foyer, and with the help of the staff, tables were arranged for the meal and we placed the large *Odeon* display panels in front of it all to screen Miss Withers and her party from the view of the other cinema patrons. Miss Withers was delighted, but as is the way of things, the manager got the accolades from head office even though it was his day off!

For many years afterwards I wrote to John and Googie, who were married in due course. My wife, Chico, and I met them in 1984 at the *Grand Theatre* in Leeds, when they were appearing in Somerset Maugham's *The Circle*. During the conversation I reminded Googie of the red cape with a hood which she had worn when we first met, and she told me then that it had been a gift from John when they had become engaged.

It was only a year or two later that the staff at the *Odeon* in Bradford received three months' salary in lieu of notice, due to the fact that the cinema was closing. It was a new building and a fine cinema, but as the years to come proved, this was no guarantee of safety, as many other cinemas suffered the same fate. As for me, I was offered and accepted the position of manager at the *Empire* cinema, just around the corner from the *Odeon*. This was a very early theatre and had recently been refurbished by Messrs Blooms of Sheffield.

Business here was good, and I knew many of the patrons from the

Arthur welcoming army cadets, members of the Territorial Army and any officer or soldier from the regular army who was on leave to the *Empire* to see a special free preview of the film *Rats of Tobruk*, starring Chips Rafferty.

Odeon. The first promotion in my newly exalted position involved a certain Miss Hebe Bliss, who was appearing in the play *Bless the Bride* at the *Alhambra Theatre* in Bradford. The film we were screening at that time was a continental musical film entitled *Rigoletto* featuring Enrico Caruso. Miss Hebe Bliss, who was eighty-two at this time, used to sing with Caruso. When she was seventeen Caruso had bought her a necklace with a gold fish pendant, and she kindly consented to appear at the cinema between performances of *Bless the*

Bride wearing this same necklace.

My next promotion involved Allan Jones, father of Jack Jones, the popular singer of the sixties and seventies. Allan was the star of the film *Firefly*, in which he sang the famous *Donkey Serenade*. He was appearing at the *Alhambra* in a big variety show, at the same time we were screening him with the Marx Brothers in *A Day at the Races*. We requested an interview with him and I proposed sending a telegram to our cinema which contained the message *My best tip for A Day at the Races, is now at the Empire Cinema* signed Allan J. I received his permission and had the resulting telegram enlarged by a local photographic studio to fit the display frame outside the cinema.

Another promotion was an easy one to work out as the film was *The Desert Rats* starring Chips Rafferty. I invited army cadets, members of the Territorial Army and any soldier on leave to show his pass and receive free admission to a preview of the film. This went down well, but so, unfortunately, did the *Empire*. It had to close and was later demolished; the site became a car park.

*Cue 6–*ON STAGE

FROM EARLY YEARS I WAS, in my own estimation, 'a nice little singer'; and whenever possible had my eyes on a career in entertainment. At odd times whilst cinema managing I had bookings as a singer with the John Marsden Orchestra at *The Rink*, Manningham Lane, Bradford. About this time I also took up tap dancing and found that 'impressions' came naturally to me. This resulted in an audition with the Eric Marsden Agency in Bradford, who got me 'spots' in shows at such prestigious venues as the Mechanics' Institute in the centre of Bradford and at National Savings rallies, singing, tap dancing and doing impressions. There was also work as Master of Ceremonies at various functions, in

The John Marsden Orchestra.

particular the radio show *Workers Playtime* which was put on at such disparate venues as the *Astra* cinema in Wakefield Road, Bradford, a large mill in Greengates, and various factories.

My act was becoming more refined and I began to specialise in Jolson impressions. It was a twenty-minute act for which I 'blacked' up. In the opening number *Alabama Bound,* I accompanied myself on the 'bones'. With what I had to offer I felt ready to try the big London agents and was eventually taken on by the Burns agency. This was run by the father of Tito Burns the orchestra leader.

As a stage act I appeared with Albert Modley, Billy Bennett, Albert Whelan, Afrique, Max Wall, Nellie Wallace, Syd Walker, Carl Barritue, Bobby Breen, David Whitfield, Leeds' 'own' Ronnie Hilton, Barry Took, Lita Roza and many more throughout many happy years on the boards, until finally quitting in 1961.

One fine act was Charles Cole the famous cartoonist, who was the creator of Elmo the Lion. He was president of the National Association of Cartoonists, and married Sophie Tucker junior, whilst appearing in *Stars in Battledress*. Unfortunately he contracted tuberculosis whilst serving in Italy during the

Arthur as Jolson during a National Savings Rally.

Arthur with Albert Modley at the *Holborn Empire*.

Star vocalist Miss Lita Roza with Arthur.

Second World War and was discharged from the Forces. He was advised that if he blew up balloons regularly this would help his recovery and by 1952 his cure was complete! How much of this was due to the balloons we shall never really know. Charles began his career as a balloon act and called himself 'Windy Blow'. He toured the world with this act which he performed in clown make-up. He lived for a while in South Yorkshire and ran a joke shop in the *Odeon Arcade*, Doncaster. He passed away in September 1986 leaving a widow and a son.

My wage in 1953 was £12 10s 0d a week while on the stage, but if I could double up a show near the theatre where I was appearing, by getting a lift with a pal, another £12 10s 0d could be earned. Membership of *Equity* was a must to get work on the stage. Sometimes, as I came off from my 'spot', the stage door keeper would inform me that my agents had called while I was 'on' to ask me to fill in a spot on a late cabaret.

One night the call came for a 'fill in' spot at the Bagatelle Restaurant in London, where the resident orchestra was Edmundo Ros and his Rumba Band. On arriving at the restaurant and enquiring where the dressing room was, I was informed that I could use the same room that Mr Ros used: it turned out to be the kitchen. Pat Kirkwood was the star of the show; but as a 'fill in' act I earned 5s a show. During the week Edmundo and I had a chance to chat. Past careers came into the conversation and whenever Edmundo and I met in the future, he always referred to me as 'the Film Man'. At the time of writing, Edmundo is now in his late eighties and lives in retirement at Hafa in Spain.

Billy Bennett was a wonderful comedian with a repertoire of outstandingly memorable monologues. Just one example of these which has stuck in my memory is:

> *Twas a dirty night, twas a dirty trick*
> *Our ship was sinking in the Atlantic.*

Edmundo Ros and his wife Britt on their wedding day.

SOS went from the wireless to the jetty
The waiter brought me onions and spaghetti.
I said to the girl 'Hang on to the buoy if you can'
She said with a coy 'Get out, you're not a buoy.
You're a dirty old man!'

Billy Bennett was a chummy, kind, heavyweight man with a unique act. For a time he joined up with Albert Whelan in a double act and they got £150 per performance between them, which was an awful lot of money in those days.

Another request from my agent was to fill in at the Shepherds Bush *Empire*, where I met with another 'fill in' called Sam Costa. He was singing with the top bands but was hoping to launch a new career as a comedian. He had a terrific moustache; and his act was both funny and clean. Following a short career as a radio presenter, he joined Dick Bentley and Kenneth Horne on the famous 'Much Binding in the Marsh', team. The star of the show we were both appearing in, was Bobby Breen from the USA. When I was a junior operator at the *Paramount* in Leeds we had screened his 1936 film *Rainbow on the River* with Jane Darwell. He was top of the bill at the *Empire* and sang five songs, all in his genuine American style. His last song was the Jolson number *Toot Toot Tootsie!* As he sang this number he rubbed two blocks of wood covered in sandpaper together to simulate the sound of a train.

Touring in early 1953 took me to the *Savoy* in Scunthorpe, where I took part in a variety show called *Showstoppers*. Our compere was Violet Pretty, a former Miss Morecambe, and the rest of the bill consisted of the Barry Sisters, an excellent blind accordionist from Grimsby called Peter Gibbs, Barry Took and myself. The top of the bill changed every two weeks, and this way I came to meet David Whitfield, Ronnie Hilton, Eddie Calvert and many more. At that time there was no shortage of work. Holiday camps were also part of our circuit and at the Scalby Mills camp in Scarborough I supported Miss Lita Roza, Carl Barritue and Afrique. I also appeared at the Lewisham *Hippodrome* alongside Reg 'Confidentially' Dixon. This was a real treat for me and about two weeks later I was fortunate to be there and appearing on the same bill as the great Max Wall. He was unique with his myriad and memorable catch phrases such as 'Thank Yew', and 'Albert; the stool, the stool!' and 'My Grandfather was the Great Wall of China - he was a brick!'. The last time we appeared at the same venue was at Morecambe. During that week the famous singing star 'Hutch' died. Max was very upset and could not work as well as he usually did. Not only had he helped Hutch to perfect his act, but they were great friends. Max Wall was a sincere man whom stardom did not change.

Morecambe was a regular venue for me during the late 1950s, and one of the more memorable occasions for me was when I appeared in the chorus of the Black and White Minstrel Show at the *Winter Gardens*. One of the soloists was Dai Francis, whose speciality in the shows was his Jolson numbers. Stan Stennett was one of the resident comedians in the show at this time. Stan and I worked together again at the Wood Green *Empire* in London. Syd and Max Harrison were two brothers who were followed into the business by their sons Hope and Keen. Max opened the act singing alone on stage. After a couple of verses Syd would rush on and shout 'Sire Cleopatra is outside,

Part of the cast from *Showstoppers* at the *Savoy*, Scunthorpe. From left to right: Barry Took, Alan Robson, Peter Gibbs and Arthur as Reg Dixon.

The Barry Sisters, one of whom was married to Alan Robson, the pianist in *Showstoppers*.

stark naked and she has not eaten for a month!' Max would reply 'Give her a good feed and send her in'; after which they went on with the act.

At that time I was appearing at the Caribbean Nite Club in Tadcaster, and so could get home to Leeds quite easily. The weather was very bad and very cold and Syd and Max were staying in a caravan on the car park near Vaux's newsagents on the Headrow. Needless to say it was freezing in the caravan, so I invited them to stay in the home Chico and I rented in Hanover Square. We were

Eddie Calvert and Arthur check on a recording used to pick up errors in performance and dialogue.

chatting in the drawing room prior to retiring for the night when who should arrive at the door but Hope and Keen who were PT instructors in the RAF at that time. Before we turned in, Syd and Max, Hope and Keen did a party piece for us which I still have on reel to reel audio tape.

1953 was the year that London was buzzing because the one and only Jimmy 'Schnozzle' Durante was appearing at the *London Palladium*. He was accompanied on this trip by his girl friend Marjorie Little and his partner of many years standing Eddie Jackson. Durante's straight man in the show was an Italian called Candy Candido with whom I had been corresponding for some years. I rang Candy and said, 'I'm not playing matinees with my act at the moment, and by showing my Equity card I can get in free to see 'Schnozzle's' matinee.' He replied, 'Give me a shout at the stage door after the matinee. I can arrange for you to meet Mr Durante.'

The matinee was terrific. The other artistes were Gillian Lynne (Ballet Suite), Rob Murray (Juggler), Harrison and Fisher (Show Dafs, which is stage slang for 'daft' - they performed silly dances), Miss Pat Kirkwood (Supreme) and, top of the bill, Jimmy Durante. It has been said that when Jimmy sang it was like a frog with a man in his throat! Jimmy closed his sixty minute slot with a song entitled *Hats*, and as the song ended Durante would say, 'Hats - I gotta

Arthur 'blacked up' for the Black and White Minstrel Show when he appeared in the chorus in Morecambe.

million,' and hats of different shapes and sizes rained down on him from above. There were about two hundred in all. All you could see of him when they stopped falling was his face and nose!

After the show I made my way to the stage door and Candy Candido took me to Durante's suite. He was lying down on the divan and sweat was just running off him. After we had been there about three minutes Candy told Durante who I was. I leaned down and shook this outstanding idol of Hollywood by the hand and congratulated him on the show. He sat up and with his large grin asked, 'How many miles have you travelled to see me?' After finding out it was about two hundred miles, Durante told Candy to give me a drink. 'Thank you, but I don't drink,' I replied.

Then he said, 'Give the guy a cigar.'

To which I had to reply, 'Sorry, but I don't smoke either.'

At that Durante said, 'Then throw the guy out!' but as this was all in fun I stayed and chatted. He was happy to note that I did impressions of him and as I was preparing to leave there was a loud knock on the door and the great Sophie Tucker dashed in. She kissed Durante and was full of praise for his act. Durante said, 'Artie, meet my best friend, Sophie Tucker.'

She shook me by the hand and half caressed me saying what a pleasure it was to meet me. Needles to say I expressed my admiration for her in response. Durante signed photographs for me and as a gesture from him, Sophie opened a smart briefcase and took out a photograph of herself and signed it for me. I have tapes from her and many letters.

In her last letter she says,' ...so sorry I'm sailing home tomorrow.' Regretfully she died shortly afterwards and is now at peace in an Israeli cemetery next to another Jewish friend of mine, Ira A Wolfe, known as 'Coffee Dan'. Another book could be written about him alone!

One fine comedian was Reg 'Confidentially' Dixon. He was top of the bill at the Finsbury Park *Empire* when I was on the same bill in much smaller letters - as it states in many contracts, 'Read the small print at the bottom'! As I usually finished my act with an impression of Reg Dixon I thought it only fair to mention this to him, so at band call I asked him if he wished me to drop this and finish up with a reprise of my opening number *I wanna say Hello!* Reg replied, 'You have said "Hello" when you opened up. You can close with the

Stan Stennett and Arthur at the Wood Green *Empire* in London.

impression of me and if I'm bad, you'll make me look good, or vice versa.'

He was a real gent. When we said goodbye he gave me his striped tie (maybe he carried a spare or two with him); but receiving this from him personally was just like receiving a 'tickling stick' from Ken Dodd! However it was not only 'goodbye' to Reg Dixon, but it was goodbye to the stage. I had decided to leave the 'Boards'. 'Living out of a suitcase' as the old saying goes, was not for me, and £12 10s.0d a week was not a lot for a family to live on.

So, at the Finsbury Park *Empire* I 'called it a day' and returned to Leeds to my wife and family. It was a return to a full daytime job but I would still be able to entertain locally. There were various charity shows, clubs and private functions where I could

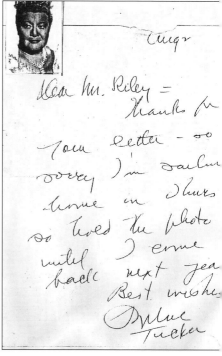

The last note Arthur received from Sophie Tucker.

still perform. I built up my 'Jolson' act and made many appearances with it on *Radio Leeds*, which at that time was in the Merrion Centre. Little did I know how *BBC Radio Leeds* was to fit into my life in later years.

Cue 7–STAR CINEMAS AND DISASTROUS CUES

EVENTUALLY I SECURED A POST as chief projectionist at the *Star Cinema* in York Road, which was not part of the chain of *Star Cinemas* despite the name. My wife Chico, worked there as chief usherette and later as cashier. Eventually she came into the projection room and worked with me.

Further up York Road was the *Shaftesbury Cinema* and it was here that I applied and was accepted for the position of assistant cinema manager. The company that ran the *Shaftesbury* was Star Cinemas of Castleford. The cinemas were only open for matinees Mondays and Saturdays, and so, on free afternoons I was able to fit in live shows at the *Grand Theatre* in Leeds. Mr F W Kaye was the house engineer at the *Grand* and would call me in along with my projectionist, Donald Smith, to work the 'limes' or to help with scene shifting alongside his full-time staff which consisted of Fred Coates, Pedro and his apprentice, who was in fact our son Jeff.

One vivid memory was of the show *Snow White and the Seven Dwarfs*. The show had gone well in the early part of the week, but one night as the dwarfs were singing *Hi Ho* whilst coming through the woods towards their house, it all went terribly wrong. The house was mounted on a turntable, which revolved to show both the exterior and the interior when necessary. One of the dwarfs had to shout, 'The lights lit,' and another had to shout back, 'The lit's light'. This was a vital cue for a blackout to occur which would enable the stage hands in the flies above the stage to hoist the scenery up to allow the house to revolve freely, but they missed the cue! As the house began to revolve, the trees were snapped to bits, making a terrible racket in the process. The dwarfs, real troopers to a man, carried on walking over the damaged scenery, throwing pieces backstage, as though it was all part of the act and a job to be done before coming home. I thought they deserved an 'Oscar'; the show went on without another 'break' but the part-time men in the flies were advised by Mr Kaye that their services would not be required again.

Another disastrous cue at the *Grand* was during a performance of *Peter Pan*. This was graded as a 'number one' show, which meant that everything had to be new from the artistes' costumes to the stage settings. One of the scenes called for Captain Hook's magnificent galleon to explode and collapse. Captain Hook was to shout, 'I will

Outside *The Rodney* at Wetherby.

rid them all of happiness,' which was supposed to be the cue for the explosion to take place. However as the actor walked on board the galleon, the explosion occurred prematurely and there was a 'black out' during which the stage cover came down. Mr Kaye, popularly known as 'Mr Rosa', was the only one authorised to set off the explosives and he had inadvertently pressed the button 'off cue'.

Mr Kaye was nicknamed 'Mr Rosa' as each morning on his way to the theatre he bought a red rose from Browne's florists. In his lapel he wore a silver sleeve which held a tiny phial of water and in this he placed his rose. For the evening shows he changed into evening dress, transferring the rose to his new outfit. He also sported a waxed moustache which went quite well with the evening dress and the rose.

Star Cinemas later asked me to take over as manager of an ancient cinema at Wetherby, called the *Rodney* which had been named after the son of one of the directors of Star Cinemas. Before refurbishment the screen at the *Rodney* had actually been painted on the wall. Star

Cinemas made the *Rodney* into Britain's finest, albeit smallest, cinemascope movie house. One morning whilst I and my handyman were outside the *Rodney* checking over certain jobs that needed to be done, a beautiful horse-drawn caravan driven by a fine gypsy man pulled up and greeted me.

He stopped and said,'I am Gipsy Petulengro, the astrologer'. He asked if it might be possible for him to site his caravan in part of the *Rodney's* car park for a couple of days' rest. After checking with the regional director of Star Cinemas, permission was duly granted.

Petulengro was happy to find a temporary base and I invited him into the office for a cup of tea and some cake. During the conversation he told me that as he was being allowed to stay on our car park, he would be happy to give free readings for any of the cinema patrons before they saw the film. Accordingly, a poster was produced informing patrons that there would be,

A free reading to all, by the one and only Gipsy Petulengro, when admission tickets are shown.

He stayed all that week and before he left he gave me a reading, and I can say, taking the good with the bad, it all came true. As he left he informed me that he had a friend who owned a black Labrador dog which, under the stage name of Viscount, could count, add, subtract and multiply any sum that he was presented with. It sounded a lovely act and so I booked them for a week. It was highly successful and as the patrons left at the end of each show they received a card with Viscount's name on it and his paw print as an autograph!

Cue 8–From Children to Adult Patronage

STAR CINEMAS PROMOTED ME and I was made the manager of the *Pavilion Cinema* at Stanningley, Leeds. The staff, having been there for a few years were well experienced, however, after about four weeks the chief projectionist, who felt that he ought to have been made the manager, came to the office and presented me with with his notice of one week. We were unaware that he had also contacted the *Pudsey News,* with the story that the *Pavilion* was soon to close and that because of this, he was leaving for a position elsewhere as projectionist. I consulted with the management of Star Cinemas about this and they replied that the man's claim was untrue. So, my first action was to counteract the projectionist's claim and a notice to this effect was placed in all the local newspapers; I then set about the business of not only keeping the existing customers but of winning additional ones. The *Pavilion* was going to be noticed.

Miss Barbara Simpson, Radio and TV star, opens the Parents Day event at the *Pavilion Cinema*, Stanningley.

David Whitfield signing autographs at the *Pavilion*.

Accordingly the *Yorkshire Evening News* reported *Novel Event - Parents Day at the Pavilion, Stanningley*. I wanted the parents to sample what the children were enjoying at the *Star's* Junior Club during the Saturday morning and matinee shows. As these special films were for members (the children), I advertised that any member who brought along a mum or a dad would be able to bring the adult in free of charge, the only cost being the usual 7d or 9d for the child members. These prices were better than pre-war days. Glen and his Grenadiers, a group, played and Parents Day was opened by Miss Barbara Simpson of Stage, TV and Radio fame. I did my Jolson numbers. The effect was to boost attendance at both children's and normal adult performances. At the start of my period at the *Pavilion* it did not have a stage, but Star Cinemas had one installed. I

Fifteen year old Helen Shapiro at the *Pavilion*.

managed to persuade such stars as David Whitfield, the fifteen year old Helen Shapiro, Stan Stennett, and Eddie Calvert to make personal appearances and sign autographs, all in the further efforts to make the membership of my Children's Club swell from 300 to 500. My years on the stage stood me in good stead here, as all our guests appeared free of charge, as they always bore in mind that their child audiences now were the adult audiences of the future.

Now more adults had to be attracted. A German film, in colour, *Arena of Fear* was to be shown. This was a circus film about the jealousy of one act of another and featured the 'Cage of Death' which was a tiger's cage. The Esso Petroleum Company let us have four

Part of the tiger poster given by Esso to support *The Arena of Fear*.

The handbill for *The Arena of Fear*.

The KOYLI tiger outside the *Pavilion* for Arena of Fear.

outsize posters of their tiger which was displayed outside with Quad posters of the film. In my younger days my father, an old soldier, had discussed army badges, regiments and their mascots with me and I remembered that the mascot of the KOYLI's (King's Own Yorkshire Light Infantry) was a tiger. I phoned the regimental headquarters, in Pontefract and contacted the commanding officer - great news! They did have a full-sized tiger (stuffed!) which was attached to a pedestal and they would be happy to loan this for the duration of the film's screening. So this also went on display inside the foyer with the posters.

Admissions began to build up! The next film was a thriller with a difference; it was entitled *The Naked Edge*, and starred Gary Cooper and Deborah Kerr. To keep up the atmosphere of expectation we approached the people who fitted traffic lights in and around the city. The reason being that, unlike at other screenings, our patrons were not going to be allowed in during the last thirteen minutes of the film, so a full set of

The handbill for *The Naked Edge* with the thirteen minute warning.

PAVILION CINEM
STANNINGLEY

Thursday, 7th Dec. for 3 d

THE NAKED EDG
starring
Gary   Debor
COOPER ★ KER

Patrons Please Note

THE RED LIGHT
outside the Cinema Entrance denote
that no one will be admitted during the
LAST 13 MINUTES OF THE FILM

STOP and enjoy a Film Thriller from the **STAR**
that will put on the **EDGE OF SUSPENS**

Gideon Shaw, Printer, Castleford.

Stewart MacGregor (centre back) British Empire Yo-Yo champion shows off one of his tricks at the *Pavilion* for the Junior (Star) Club members. With him (left to right) Mr Heptonstall (head of Cinema Clubs, Star Cinemas), Leslie Parker (club member), David Griffith (club member) Arthur Riley (cinema manager).

traffic lights were installed just outside the main doors. At the start of the last fifteen minutes a button was pressed and the red lights came on. Alongside the lights a notice was placed which read, *Stop and enjoy a film thriller from the start that will put you on the edge of suspense.* Again we had full houses.

The Junior (Star) Club's next surprise was to be entertained by the Yo-yo champions of the world; one was a Canadian called Steve

Rider, and the other was the British champion, Stewart MacGregor. These two could do fifty to sixty tricks with Yo-yos, and it did the trick for us too. One promotion for the film *The Clown and the Kids*, won acclaim when clowns from the Bertram Mills Circus visited and, on the lawn in front of the cinema, performed many of their circus tricks. One side of the *Pavilion* was adjacent to the main road that linked Leeds and Bradford. There were bus stops on both sides of the road, and so all the people waiting at the stops or passing on the buses, could not miss what was going on for the entertainment of the boys and girls of the Star Junior Club.

Norman Wisdom's outstanding film *On the Beat* was a great event and real fun to take part in. With the permission of the chief constable of Leeds, Mr A V Patterson, uniformed police were on duty

Clowns from the Bertram Mills Circus perform outside the *Pavilion Cinema*, Stanningley for *The Clown and the Kid*.

Staff and police on duty for the promotion of *On the Beat*. (Left to right) Miss M E Foster, police dummy, Miss Fowler, police cadet Alan Burnett and Miss Pollard.

in the foyer at the evening shows. We also had a dummy policeman and policewoman there. There was an hilarious event when Norman Wisdom came to the *Pavilion* and was shown by a policeman, two patrons and several of the children, the correct procedure for crossing a road and how to use a pedestrian crossing! The result as you may imagine was anarchic. The poster for this event read, *Use this crossing and keep alive to visit the Pavilion.*

To boost the *Pavilion's* profile further I had a large glazed frame on strong legs erected on our property adjacent to the bus stop, and in this was displayed a poster with the heading *Look Who's Been Here* with signed photographs of those celebrities from stage and screen

Norman Wisdom at the time of *On The Beat*.

who had paid us a visit. Edmundo Ros had judged a 'Winter Photography' competition and a local ballerina, Gillian Wood of Pudsey, had broken off her holiday to appear in person to promote the film *Flower Drum Song*. The *Pavilion* was also visited by Jimmy Saville, early on in his career. Jimmy arrived in a borrowed Austin Princess and was dressed in a dark suit and

Jimmy Saville visiting the *Pavilion*.

Gillian Wood of Pudsey, who helped promote *The Flower Drum Song*.

The Twist competition to promote *Rock Around the Clock*. Centre Jackie, who demonstrated the dances and the winner of the competition, four year old Darien Payne.

a white stetson hat. This hat was one of Jimmy's first gimmicks.

A very talented dancer named Jackie, from Half Mile Lane in Stanningley, fronted and led a Twist competition to support the film *Rock Around the Clock*. Jackie demonstrated many different contemporary dances and then the audience voted for the winner from the children who had taken part in the Twist competition. It was won by a young four year old girl named Darien Payne of Sommerfield Road, Bramley.

Now the *Pavilion* was being noticed by young and old alike and I put a proposal forward to the

Arthur and some of his usherettes on the steps of the Pavilion.

Mrs Leaf, kiosk sales at the Pavilion.

company, suggesting that on Sunday nights all seats would be 5s (25p). We would screen two big films, and have a group on the stage. The audiences on Sunday nights continued to grow, however, the regional manager then informed me, that the company intended to put on Bingo from 2.00pm to 4.00pm on Sundays. As the shows were due to start at 5.00pm, that did not leave us much time for sweeping out the cinema for the film audiences. His answer was to the effect that it could all be done in an hour easily!

A number of weeks passed by with Sunday afternoon Bingo, but it was not a great success even though a 'Full House' and the Jackpot totalled £87, which was a lot of money in those days. To try and boost the numbers, my old pal David Whitfield, who was appearing in *Sleeping Beauty* at the *Grand Theatre*, Leeds, came up one Sunday to present the winning cash. I was far from pleased when we began to get people in from the nearby pub the *Waggon and Horses*, as it took a while to get them settled and the staff did not have enough time after the Bingo session to clean out the cinema and have a meal break. As film time drew near, some of the staff were still eating whilst on duty. None of us cared for this, least of all me and on a visit by the regional manager a few days later I mentioned this to him. 'Well Mr Riley, if you are not satisfied I can soon replace you. Seven times you have been top manager in my area, but this does not make you indispensable.'

My immediate response was to sit at my desk, write out my notice and to hand it to him. I did regret leaving the *Pavilion* and its loyal staff, after all that hard work we had put in. Some time after I left,

Arthur and his front of house staff in the foyer of the *Pavilion* December 1961.

the *Pavilion* closed as a cinema; it became a Bingo hall, warehouse and a sports gym. It has now been converted into offices. As for me, I took over as manager of the *Hyde Park Cinema* in Brudenell Road, Leeds.

Cue 9–HYDE PARK CORNER

THE MOVE TO THE *HYDE PARK CINEMA,* meant that I was
working for a family rather than a company. Mr L Shann and his wife
Ann owned the cinema and their daughter Doreen acted as the
business secretary. I was at the *Hyde Park Cinema* for six years. Whilst
there I managed to negotiate the loan of a full-sized elephant called
Burma from Billy Smart's Circus, which was encamped at the time

**Burma the elephant, on loan from Billy Smart's Circus, arrives at
the *Hyde Park Cinema* to promote *The Big Hunt*.**

on Woodhouse Moor. I needed Burma to help me promote a film entitled *The Big Hunt*. I will never forget the meeting I had with Billy Smart and his wife in their Royal Windsor caravan; In exchange for Burma's services we agreed to hold a midnight show of the film for all the circus acts, with the Elephant Boy from the circus. We walked Burma down to the *Hyde Park Cinema* where a hundred or so families were eagerly waiting to be entertained by him.

A new pop sensation at this time was a good-looking young man called Cliff Richard, and he had made a film called *Espresso Bongo*, and the *Hyde Park* won the right to show this black and white film for its premiere in Leeds. Cliff was in the States but was due back to appear at the *Empire Theatre* in Leeds, so I contacted his public relations office and enquired if he could pay us a personal visit during his time in Leeds. A reply was received that, due to unforeseen circumstances, Cliff would not be able to appear personally at the *Hyde Park*, but the entire Shann family were invited to meet him and see the show. He also sent me 150 of his records to be given out to patrons of the *Hyde Park*. Jimmy Saville was invited to visit the cinema and to give out the discs and chat about Cliff, who at that time was a great chum of his. Jimmy arrived in his new car; he had by this time graduated to a sporty Jaguar. The audience loved it.

Bernard Miles, my friend from the 1940s, had gone on to found the *Mermaid Theatre* in London after the war, and one of the Directors of this theatre was the film actor Leo Genn. Genn was also a great personal friend of Bernard's. He was appearing at the *Grand Theatre*, Leeds in a play about the Maquis, the French underground during the war. At the same time we were showing a war film at the *Hyde Park* entitled *No Time to Die*, in which Leo Genn had a strong part, starring in it alongside Bonar Colleano who had sadly been killed in a car crash. I went down to the *Grand* and presented my card at the stage door. On the card I wrote that I was a friend of Bernard Miles and would Mr Genn consent to see me. The answer came back, 'Yes.' Leo Genn was a gentleman as well as being a big star. He wanted to know how I had met Bernard, and I told him and let him look through the letters from Bernard that I had brought with me. After looking through them he asked my reasons for wanting to see him. The answer was of course 'Promotion.' After explaining that we were showing his film I asked him if he could pay us a visit to help in publicising it. He was delighted, but explained that he had a very tight schedule. However he wrote the initials NTTD (No Time to Die) in red greasepaint on his dressing room mirror.

Leo Genn arrives at the *Hyde Park* to promote *No Time to Die*.

He continued, 'But look, Arthur, if you are willing to wait in your office until I ring you, yes or no, then it will be a deal one way or the other.'

Naturally I agreed to this, and having been given a signed photograph, I bade him good morning and took my leave.

On my return to the *Hyde Park* I arranged for a poster to be made ready to go up outside the moment he agreed, to the effect that Leo Genn would be making a personal appearance. A local photographer was also put on standby by to be ready at a moment's notice to come round and photograph his arrival. All I had to do now was to wait for the phone to ring

Leo Genn inspecting the display used to promote *No Time to Die*.

with a 'yes' from Mr Genn. It got to Wednesday about 5.00pm before the phone did ring and a lady's voice said she was speaking on behalf of Mr Genn and that he could appear for fifteen minutes on the Thursday evening. The lady who rang was Mrs Genn! As the film was on for a week it was a great help towards boosting the takings. The poster, with the date and time inserted, was put outside and the photographer informed. At 5.30pm on the Thursday, Leo Genn and his wife arrived in a chauffeur driven car. He declined a drink and said he would chat with the patrons, have photographs taken, and then make his way to the *Grand Theatre*. I was very grateful for his participation in this excellent promotion.

At a later date, when going through the forthcoming monthly programme I was slightly dismayed to see that one film, *Harry Black*, starring Stewart Grainger was on the schedule. This film had previously been the rounds of every other cinema in Leeds before coming to us. Mr Shann professed his confidence in my ability to sell it and promptly left. After some thought, my favourite animal, the tiger, came once again to my rescue. The story of the film centred on a tiger. I had borrowed a real elephant for *The Big Hunt*, but I did not think that I would be allowed to borrow a real tiger, even if the circus was in town at the time; so once again I contacted the commanding officer at the KOYLI (King's Own Yorkshire Light Infantry)

Chico and the KOYLI mascot used to promote Harry Black.

headquarters in Pontefract and was allowed to borrow their mascot once again.

The film was to be screened over a bank holiday period and patrons had to be lured away from other venues and attractions. A large poster was made up to go alongside the tiger in the entrance reading,

> *This is the target of Harry Black, game hunter; my target for your holiday is Harry Black starring Stewart Grainger on …*

and showed the dates. The tiger was put on show outside the entrance and the families flocked in. They were thrilled to be able to stroke a real tiger in safety, even if it was a stuffed one! My last and hardest promotion at the *Hyde Park* was for the film *Ali Baba and the Forty Thieves* which was in colour. The *Hyde Park* was fortunately patronised by students from the nearby Leeds University, and after

One of the models used outside the *Hyde Park* to promote *Ali Baba and the Forty Thieves*.

Arthur with some of the staff at the *Hyde Park*.

talking to one student of Oriental Culture it was arranged that, in exchange for free tickets for a couple of future films, he would write down thirty-nine oriental names, both male and female. The competition was for the patrons to guess the name of the fortieth of Ali Baba's thieves and win the prize. Ben Shaw's of Halifax were introducing a new drink at the time called Irn-Bru, and I put the suggestion to them that Irn Bru would be a good name to use for the fortieth thief. They agreed and provided a crate of all of their drinks as a prize for the winner. I had a huge card made showing all the forty names. The caption read that the first patron to spot the odd one out would receive a prize. As it happened only one patron spotted the name. Large papier mâché models of Ali Baba had been made to go either side of the promotion banner above the door and these too caused a lot of comment. A short while later Mr Shann died, and the cinema was taken over by another company who wanted to place their own manager in. It was a sad day when I had to say goodbye to my faithful staff at the *Hyde Park*.

*Cue 10–*A CHANGE OF LIFESTYLE

WITH THE DEATH OF MR SHANN and Bingo taking over in those cinemas that were not flourishing, I had to look outside the cinema industry for my next job. After an interview I was offered a position as forecourt and petrol attendant at Arnold G Wilson Limited, Moortown Garage. Arnold G Wilson's were a prestigious car dealership in Leeds at this time and the Moortown Garage was situated across the road from the *Chained Bull* public house Coincidentally, the landlord of the *Chained Bull* at this time was one Henry Croudson who had played the organ when I was a trainee projectionist at the *Paramount Theatre*. Work at the garage was organised on a shift pattern, but the pay was good and there were the tips from the motorists when we checked that the car's battery, oil and water was topped up. We also cleaned the windscreen if we had

Moortown Garage: Bob, Arthur and Jim.

time and in that way I met many of the leading Leeds business men, surgeons, solicitors, market and fair traders. The manager of the garage was Mr Colin McLay, and neither he, nor his deputy, interfered with us as long as the department was running smoothly.

The secretary at the garage was Shirley Haines whose husband Guy worked further down the parade. Guy and I found we had a lot in common as he too had been a cinema projectionist. The Haineses became long-standing family friends as Guy, like myself, owned 16mm sound projectors. We exchanged films, ideas and also gave film shows together; sometimes for charity and sometimes for payment. Donisthorpe Hall, the retirement home for aged Jewish folk, which was just around the corner from the garage, was one of our playgrounds for film shows. *The Jolson Story* was one of the residents' favourites but we showed many more assorted films there. Mr Black, a customer at the garage, was one of the main committee members at the Blind School for Jewish people in Street Lane, which was also not far from the garage. Occasional Sundays found me there when I presented a show called *Record Times*, a programme of popular music from disc.

Shirley Haines and Guy Haines.

One day whilst on duty at the petrol pumps a 'Riley 9' black soft-top car pulled up for petrol and a service. On first hearing the driver speak, I thought he was from the United States as he asked me to, '...fill her up with gasoline and see to me tyres and that.' Thinking that I was the owner he then said, 'You own a nice little outfit here, and friendly.' He paid, and included a generous tip and told me that his name was Naylor, and that he was Canadian and was head of the Canadian Immigration Service in Leeds. His office was in Station House, near the railway station in Leeds. Before leaving he asked, 'Say, do you know any person who has a mobile 16mm sound projector?' Did I know!

He was surprised and pleased when he learnt that I had two 16mm projectors of my own. He then handed me his card and said, 'We'll make arrangements for shows; you gotta come to our flat in Shadwell Lane,' which was once again only around the corner from the garage. We arranged to meet at a later date and at this meeting he told me that he gave lectures to people who were thinking of emigrating to Canada, and he wanted to know if I would be willing to show the films he had brought on my projector. I mentioned to him that my friend Guy also had projectors, and that if ever I was not able to do a show at any time, Guy would be only too happy to stand in. As it turned out we often did the shows together. One time, whilst Guy and I were setting up, a call came in from Mr Naylor. It was only ten minutes before we were due to start and he had been unavoidably detained. He asked if I would, '...open the chat talk to the folks that were waiting.' I duly delivered the lecture and Guy screened the films. Mr Naylor was in Leeds for about eighteen months before moving on to Denver, Colorado.

You never know just who you will serve on a forecourt. At various times whilst on duty, I served Dusty Springfield and Danny Williams. Williams was a young South African singer who was performing at the Moortown Corner Night Club, just across the road from the garage. The continual flow of customers kept me busy during the day and Guy and I were happy to go out in the evenings with a film show, or I would go entertaining; either paid, or for charity. Another customers was Rabbi Brown from the local synagogue, and during one conversation he asked if a very special film he had seen entitled *Hand in Hand* could be obtained on 16mm sound. *Hand in Hand* was the story of a Jewish boy and a Catholic girl whose pets had died. The children had to make a decision on how to send them to God, so 'hand in hand' they make their decisions. As I was working when the film was finally delivered, Guy went along with his two projectors and a large mixed audience viewed the film at Leeds University. Rabbi Brown praised Guy on a good show, with an excellent film which had delighted everyone,

One large car that came in regularly was owned by a Mr Landy. In the late fifties and early sixties Whit Sunday mornings were fairly quiet as there was not much traffic about so I could clearly hear a car horn blowing continuously from just below the *Chained Bull*. I saw that it was Mr Landy's car, which was out of control and Mr Landy himself was slumped over the steering wheel. Fortunately the car was not travelling fast, but it was zig-zagging about and seemed to be heading straight for the forecourt. It just missed us and so I ran after it and managed to open the driver's door. Fortunately the car was of the type where the handbrake was sited on the right hand side of the driver and I managed to put this on. The car had nearly stopped now but it ran on a little and was finally stopped by a tree outside a shop. Mr Landy was still conscious and managed to point to a pocket in his blazer where I found a bottle. In response to his signal, I took out a tablet and put it in his mouth. He had identification on him and I was able to get his home telephone number from that, and after running back to the garage I phoned his wife. Of course she was very upset, and told me her son would soon be there, which he was. Mr Landy had a heart condition and if I had not been *on cue* he might have died. Though very soon I was to change my lifestyle again, Guy and I continued to make our own cinemas at home and with 16mm sound, record and tapes we enjoyed our hobby immensely.

Arthur at home in his den with his beloved Siemens and Debrie projector.

Cue 11–TALKING AND SELLING TO FRATERNITY AND MECCA

IT WAS A CUSTOMER who used the garage regularly who caused my life to take a different direction, and once again it was a change that called for all the training that life on the stage had given me. Mr Harris drove a Rolls Royce that was always immaculate and his usual greeting was, 'Hello Arthur! Do the lot please.' He was always most grateful, paid promptly and left a good tip. One day as he was about to drive off, he shouted me round to the driver's side of the car and handed me his card.

You can sell yourself and the products. Go to this address in Bradford. There's a job for you there working for me.

He mentioned the salary which was most acceptable so, on my next

Super Save Salesrooms at Doncaster.

2.129. HALL GATE, DONCASTER.

day off, I went over to Bradford. Mr Harris, known as Gaby to his chums, owned salesrooms in Bradford, York and Doncaster and I was to be one of the fast-selling salesmen working from a rostrum with a team of sales girls and cashiers for the Super Save Salesrooms. My stage experience meant that I could project the company image and I could talk and had plenty of confidence. The salesmen had to be well dressed and smartly turned out. The salary was very good and the bonuses which topped it up made it the best paid job I had ever had!

As it was a major mining town, Mr Harris had taken the decision to open the Doncaster salesroom until 9.30pm. The late opening time was a major attraction and fitted in with the shift changes at the pits. There were the occasional hitches however. One night, as dusk was falling, the electricity failed and we were plunged into darkness. Nonetheless the rostrum we sold from was next to the main windows and the lights in the adjacent arcade shone in through it, lighting up the rostrum like a spotlight. To liven up what could have been a poor evening for selling I sang some well-known ditties, my own song *I Wanna Say Hello*, as well as Reg Dixon's *Confidentially*. We managed to fill the salesroom which held over three hundred people. Mr Harris and the other partners listened in over the telephone. They all thought it was an excellent sale and my wage packet reflected his appreciation.

The York salesroom attracted many tourists who were intrigued by our fast way of selling. The goods were all genuine products and top-line names, but they were bought in bulk at a substantial discount and then sold direct to the retail customer at prices which were cheaper than most shops, but marked up to give a modest profit on each sale. Our profit came from the sheer volume of sales. After a number of weeks at York, I was approached by a gentleman who introduced himself as the manager of the *ABC Regal Cinema* which was situated just round the corner from our salesroom. They had heard that I was an entertainer and asked if it might be possible for me to entertain at the *Regal* for the Junior Club each Saturday morning from 9.30am to 10.30am. Happily Mr Harris thought it was a fine idea, and we arranged for a trainee salesman to do the early slot each Saturday morning whilst I slipped round to the *Regal*. It was a real delight and an ideal warm-up for my selling during the rest of the day.

One week in 1969 the *Regal* was to show the film *The Italian Job* and the manager asked if I had any ideas for promoting this. I asked the manager to arrange with the police for clearance of the area in

The stunt for *The Italian Job* in Main Street, York.

front of the cinema so that there was room for myself dressed like a Mafia hood, a Mini and our big Super Save van. I wanted to recreate a stunt from the film. In the film the thieves in a Mini drive up two metal runners into the back of a moving van in a spectacular getaway. The police would not let us duplicate this exactly so, there was me in an Italian straw hat, black suit and dark glasses jumping into a Mini and driving up into our stationary van; once in the van Roy, our driver, drove off at speed. We had a large poster pasted to either side of the van which read: 'On loan for *The Italian Job* - see the action next week at the *ABC Regal*.' So naturally all the bystanders saw this. The manager of the *Regal* was awarded a trophy for the promotion.

We worked a rota at the different salesrooms and on one occasion I was at the Bradford salesroom. This was the base of two of the partners Mr Mick Connolly and of Mr Dobbs, an ex-Leeds city policeman, who attended to all the security arrangements from the Bradford office. One morning Mr Dobbs called me into the office.

'Your wife's on the phone; seems upset'. When I spoke to her she said, 'Arthur, you didn't warn me you were leaving me.'

Somewhat shocked to say the least I asked her why she thought that I was, and it appeared that a letter had arrived from Leeds and Bradford Airport requesting that I collect the pink Antler suitcase that I had left prior to my departure for the United States. This was a shock to me too; so assuring Chico that I would sort it out, I rang off and told Mr Dobbs. He reassured me and said, 'You and I will check it out on Sunday.'

When Sunday came, armed with the letter, Mr Dobbs and myself arrived at Leeds and Bradford Airport, and after presenting the letter we passed through Security and arrived at a counter marked 'Valuables'. The Security Guard asked the young lady there to pass me my supposed suitcase.

It took a great deal of effort to lift it down to me. 'This is not my suitcase' I told them, but the guard replied, 'It has your name and address inside sir!'

At this he lifted the lid and revealed the contents. The suitcase was full of mink furs, jewellery, dresses and costumes and on the top of it all a 10 inch by 8 inch brown envelope with my address written on it in clear block letters. In a flash it came to me; at that time I was corresponding with a man named Roger Barrett who was an expert in voice-overs for films and he was married at the time to Jane Russell, the Hollywood film star. I informed the security man that the case belonged to Miss Jane Russell.

Mr Dobbs looked at me as much as to say, 'Arthur, what sort of publicity stunt are you pulling now?' After assuring Airport Security that I had Miss Russell's home address and would be responsible for returning it to her, I signed for the case and, accompanied by Mr Dobbs, returned to my home. The police had to be called because of the gold items in the suitcase as well as the many other personal items belonging to Miss Russell, which even included her night wear. My wife could not believe it; would yours?

Little did we know that at the same time that we had collected the suitcase Roger Barrett had suffered a heart attack which resulted tragically in his death. Jane Russell was informed by telegram the following day and we received a response immediately. A letter followed telling how the suitcase had been lost. Tommy, one of the children Jane had adopted in London, was making his way back to the States with a group; Jane had told him to bring the suitcase back with his baggage but the airline had wanted to charge excess baggage for it. Tommy did not have the money so he put the suitcase on hold,

Jane Russell and Robert Mitchum photographed at Jane's wedding to Roger Barrett.

and then had promptly forgotten all about it! Jane requested me to return the suitcase and its contents via a carrier from the airline for which she would pay.

Jane was, of course, upset over the death of her husband but managed to say, 'If Roger was alive he would have laughed over this,' but then she said, 'Thank the Lord above that my suitcase was found by an honest person.'

Jane was a very religious person, and many photographs and letters have passed between her and myself since this comical event. We continued to correspond and she invited all the Riley's, to go over for a two week holiday at her expense. We were thrilled and once again we had a promotion for the Bradford salesroom with poster and banners inside and out reading,

Arthur, your favourite salesman, offers special sales before departing to the USA to visit his friend, Jane Russell.

Sales were very good as a result. Arrangements were made for all the family to fly out four weeks before Christmas, and we were all looking forward to it when disaster struck. The head salesman died suddenly, and my promotion to his position meant that I had to do three salesrooms in a week, those of Bradford, York and Doncaster. This unfortunately meant that we had to cancel our trip, and I had to inform Jane. One of her representatives from London called on me and delivered Jane's Christmas presents to us all. Since then Jane has remarried but writes to me regularly. In 1997 her close friend Robert Mitchum died, which upset her terribly. Since adopting Tommy, who was from London, Jane has found homes for over 20,000 children, mostly handicapped all over the world. Her third husband is John Peoples, which I think is rather appropriate with all of Jane's people, all the orphans she has helped.

At the Super Save Salesrooms most of the items we sold came from overseas, Russian radios, Phillips imports from Holland and such. The Government began to impose tight import restrictions which meant that one salesroom had to close and York was chosen. Sadly Mr Gaby Harris passed away, aged only about fifty-five, following which, one by one the other salesrooms were sold.

However the management asked me to manage a Prize Bingo Club, the Fraternity at Meanwood. This paved the way for me to apply to Mecca in London to obtain a similar position with them based at the Dominion Bingo and Social Club in Chapel Allerton, Leeds, where again my stage and cinema experience stood me in good stead. I didn't realise then that I would be with them for fourteen years! With Mecca it was 'go-go-go!' The Miss World contest was then also run by the group. Everyone worked hard to promote the club and attract more and more customers. With double sessions we could attract about 1,600 people each night.

Like my cinema and stage career, my job with Mecca was to be a full-time position, again with unsocial hours. Audiences were a different mixture, being mainly ladies; the social Bingo club was an escape from their household chores. As these audiences were with you afternoon and evening, there was a doubling up on the jobs to be done. I did not mind this, but soon found that I was not a natural as a barman, as due to my cinema life I did not drink or smoke, and this left a gap between me and the customers that I could not readily bridge.

From time to time the managers had promotional ideas. Easter time, Pancake Tuesday and such were easy to promote. However, they realised that my promotional ideas tended to be of a different and wide-ranging nature, so they gave me a free hand. Eric Morley, the director of Mecca, also owned the rights to the Miss World contest, so all the staff were briefed on who the current Miss World was, and which part of the world she came from. As part of her years duties the current Miss World would visit us and when the interval came the manager would bring her down the aisle on his arm. She would be introduced to the audience, say a few words, then off stage and away. We did, of course, have an extra Miss World Bingo game in her honour on these occasions.

In 1976 a young lady from the Caribbean, Cindy Braikwaite, was chosen as Miss World. At that time she was dating the late Bob Marley. The manager requested me to make it a day to remember for her, so the promotion was to be a day of Carnival. We asked the club members to dress in carnival fashion if they wished, and arranged for lots of tropical fruit to be around. The members certainly responded and were filled with the carnival spirit. A local steel band came along and the stage, theatre and auditorium were filled with a fine array of banners. streamers and balloons. We even borrowed some palm trees from a furniture store in Leeds. They were filthy from being in store when they were collected, but we washed them down in the car park, much to the amusement of passing motorists, pedestrians and especially children. Once on stage and under the lights they looked most effective. The fruit had been provided by stallholders from Leeds Market, and after the event it was all taken to St James's Hospital and given out to the patients.

Preparations were well in hand, and many club members were only too willing to lend a hand. It was a Social Club indeed. Larry Spence, one of the members, had previously done a marvellous mime to the record *Speedy Gonzales*. He was only a small chap, and with a large sombrero hat on his head and a rug around his shoulders he agreed to squat near a stock of fruit and pretend to be having a siesta. On the day, at a cue from me, the steel band struck up and with myself dressed in a white suit and straw hat, I got the audience to mamba, tango and shuffle round the aisles to the top door at the rear of the theatre. As arranged, Miss World joined in the dance and made her way to the stage where she received a terrific round of applause.

She was chatting to everyone when I shouted,'Hey, where's Speedy? Asleep again! Hey Speedy!' at which Larry stood up and did his *Speedy Gonzales* act. Cindy Braikwaite was delighted and as Larry finished she kissed his cheek, took up a pineapple and gave it to him.

Cindy Breakwaite, Miss World, with Arthur.

Cue 12–PROMOTIONS

MOVIES, MUSIC AND PROMOTIONS still meant a lot to me so a *Hollywood Nite* was a must. All the members were requested to come as their idol from the films and the response was terrific. Members came in to music entitled *Hollywood Hits*. My main concern was who was I to portray. I decided to portray Gypsy Rose Lee. I had never done 'drag' before but my wife Chico, as always, was on hand to help in the transformation. Though I did not have too much hair on my head, a hair net was used to hold it in position. Next she made me up with bright lipstick and false eyelashes. Then came the wig. Two oranges were tucked into a smart bra to give me the required shape. For the first time in my life I wore fish-net stockings which were held in position with paper clips for safety, then I stepped into the costume. It was salmon pink with silver and gold ornamentation. A three foot high head-dress, like those seen in the

Arthur's Hollywood Nite costume.

Follies Bergere or a big Las Vegas show topped off the ensemble. Lastly there were the sparkling ladies' dance shoes. A tape played a fanfare introduction, and I did a voice over, 'Hi there folks, Miss Gypsy Rose Lee is here is person.' and walked out on stage. There I sang two songs *A Pretty Girl is Like a Melody* and *Always* .

A full house assured good prize money and a special 'Hollywood' game was played, with again a good pay out. One of the ladies had made a lovely Carmen Miranda outfit with a wonderful 'tutti frutti' hat decorated with plastic fruit and I was thrilled when, after the show, she gave the hat to me in case I should ever do 'drag' again. I was soon called upon to do so. There was much scope for more nights like this, as full houses resulted in

Complete with Tutti Frutti hat, Arthur as Carmen Miranda.

good bonuses for staff as well as good prize money for the patrons.

We were always having special afternoons where senior citizens were entitled to free sandwiches, teacakes and a spirited 'flyer' for them, making them feel special. The cafe staff laid on a full buffet and my wife would help serve tea to those who were not so mobile. Mecca arranged a special Bingo Rally at Great Horton in Bradford, and put on free coaches for all those patrons who wished to go along one Sunday morning. The fun and games were to commence at 12.00noon with special bingo games to start at 1.00pm.

A message came down that 'Arthur will be responsible for all the entertainment', though they had already booked a group *Black Onyx*. I took along the Carmen Miranda outfit and opened up the afternoon by miming to two numbers being played on a tape; then, to more Latin American, I got everyone up, members and staff alike, and, weaving in and out of the tables, we recreated a real carnival scene. Free sandwiches and tea cakes were served for all members and staff and then *Black Onyx* did their spot. They were stylish, with clear vocals and good instrumentals. One of the group took off Shirley Bassey whilst singing *This is my Life*, and they ended with a good old fashioned sing-a-long.

At the *Dominion* we learnt that one of our oldest members, Mrs

Lavinia Knowles, would soon be ninety. We requested birthday cards for her from other members when this date came round, and it was gratifying to see, as each day went by, more and more cards arriving. Mecca arranged a ninetieth birthday party for her, with free bubbly for all to drink her health in a toast. We kept our fingers crossed for her continued good health and informed her family of what we were planning for their mother's birthday. All around the display area on the stage, ninety cards were fixed (even though we actually received 117). Lavinia and her family duly arrived at the *Dominion*, and got a bigger welcome than any Miss World. I presented her with a huge floral tribute which joined the others from her family. Lavinia lived to see her hundredth birthday.

In the fourteen years that I was with Mecca I worked with a number of managers who were trained in the Mecca way. They were good with figures and the games were plotted as the company required. It was rather gratifying therefore when a young man who had arrived as manager told me that he had previously been an assistant in a superstore, but that:

Mrs Lavina Knowles, the *Dominion's* oldest member, being presented with flowers on behalf of the management and staff of Mecca on her 90th birthday.

Mr Bingham informed me if I wanted to know about the members, promotions and events, then Arthur will guide you through. He's like an Ambassador at the Dominion!

This particular manager, Mr Lindley, was someone who would put himself out to help both members and staff, and therefore I wanted to put on a promotion to show him how things worked between myself, the staff and the members. It was not near any of the usual promotion periods such as Easter or Christmas, so he was intrigued when I asked him if he felt like being a Mad Hatter. I got the reply 'Like you? Yes Arthur,' so I plotted a Mad Hatter's Tea Party. This would not be held at the *Dominion*, but in one of the children's wards of St James's Hospital.

Throughout my career, I used Homburgs Theatrical Suppliers in Leeds and managed to obtain through them a Mad Hatter's suit for Mr Lindley, and Diane, the head security cashier was to be Alice; guess who got to be the White Rabbit! An appeal was put out from the stage for donations of chocolates, sweets and the like, and members responded in their usual generous way. In fact we could have opened a sweet shop of our own! To complete the party I felt

The Mad Hatter's Teaparty, (left to right) George as the Milky Bar Kid, Bob Lindley as the Mad Hatter, Diane as Alice and guess who as the White Rabbit!

that we ought to have some character to whom the children could relate. Someone like the Milky Bar Kid. Our doorman was a small man aged sixty-seven but he asked, 'Arthur, can I play the Milky Bar Kid?'

'Sure,' I said, so we kitted him out in cowboy gear. Now you can't have a Milky Bar Kid without some Milky Bars to give out, so I had a word with the owner of Grant's sweet and tobacco shop across the road, asking if he would let us have a dozen boxes of Milky Bars at a reduced price. Mr Grant replied that as our members had been coming in to buy the sweets and chocolates for the hospital treat from him, then the least he could do was give me three dozen boxes! A very generous gesture.

We had so many goodies when we arrived, that all the children's wards at St James's were visited and sweets given out to every one. It was a successful introduction for Mr Lindley who made the front page of the *Yorkshire Evening Post* in his Mad Hatter suit, holding a baby!

Cue 13–Cars, Independence Day and Irish Dancers

AS A DIVERSION FROM MY WORK with Mecca, I occasionally used my flair for publicity for other companies and in 1980 was approached by a previous employer, Arnold G Wilson Limited, to help with the launch of the new car, the Austin Metro. After discussions with the general manager of the Horsforth branch, I went up to the showroom to set up the display. Afterwards I received a very kind letter from him with a record voucher for a generous amount, which, needless to say, with my love of music was put to very good use.

There were further promotions for me to 'cut into slot' at Mecca and ironically soon after the Metro launch the *Dominion* was to put on a game, with the prize being a new Ford car. We were let down by the makers who were to deliver the vehicle for display on the night, so I went on stage and asked if any member had such a car. One did and agreed to loan it to us for our promotion.

Mecca did not issue instructions that everything had to be

The Ford Car promotion at the *Dominion*.

The
D
O
M
I
N
I
O
N

Mecca Social Club
Harrogate Road Leeds 7. Tel. 621679

* Delightful Surroundings
* Open every afternoon and evening
* Meet and make friends
* Interesting and different
* Never a dull moment
* In place to go
* Only 20p admission
* Now come along and join them

The friendliest people in Leeds!

JIMMY (THE MANAGER) AND HIS STAFF

special features

READY TO WELCOME YOU

WITH STAR GUESTS (MISS WORLD '76)

● LICENSED BAR AFTERNOON & EVENING
● MEMBERS ONLY (OVER 18)

HOME BAKED PRODUCE ON BUFFET ●
MEMBERSHIP FORMS AVAILABLE ON REQUEST ●

A promotional flyer for the *Dominion*.

celebrated or a full promotion slotted in, but we all had to make the customers aware of the special games, where exciting holidays abroad or cruises on the QE2, were the prizes. One special occasion which I drew to the customers' attention was Remembrance Day. Chico had volunteered to help with the allocation and collection of the boxes from the volunteers, who were selling poppies on behalf of the British Legion and as a result I had met Mr Banks, who was the chief officer of the British Legion in Leeds. Even though no special collections were allowed to be made on Mecca premises, I did eventually obtain permission to put on a suitable stage show at the *Dominion* near the 11 November. The banners and flags of each Legion area were fixed above the façade of the stage, and we played suitable music and military marches. I even had the band of the Sea Cadets playing on stage and one year Guy Haines brought his sound projector and screened films on the new tanks and armoured vehicles that the British Army were using. Like other film shows that Guy had screened it went down well, after all the *Dominion* had been a beautiful cinema. It had opened in January 1934 with the film *Cleaning Up* starring George Gee, and was only closed during the war years because of a fire in 1941. By 1953 it had been re-furbished and opened for business, though sadly it closed on 18 March 1967 after showing *The Quiller Memorandum* starring George Segal, George Sanders and Alec Guinness. Mecca bought it for £65,000 and Bingo took over, but in March 1988 demolition work began on the *Dominion* site and as I write, flats are being built there. It was a bingo hall for twenty-nine years.

One of the big items in our promotion portfolio was Independence

The White Roses, a barbershop ensemble based in Leeds.

Arthur as Uncle Sam for the 4 July celebration, signed by James Cagney in bottom right corner.

Day, that is the 4 July. Enquiries were made from Mecca headquarters about our willingness to join in and what our plans were regarding attracting our members in during this promotion. Music, of course was to play a part. From the collection of tapes that I had at home we arranged a *Yankee Doodle* session of ceremonial music from the States. The city of Leeds was also the home of an outstanding group of barbershop singers known as the *White Roses*. They had over twenty years' experience of singing to audiences all over the world. Their companion group known as the *White Rosettes*, was made up of ladies who, like the male section, carried away many top awards. Founded by Clive and Sandra Landy, the members of both groups were drawn from diverse occupations and areas of residence. Dot Saunders, who came from Liverpool, was the inspiration behind the formation of the Rosettes.

Now we had our theme, the staff rallied round and dressed in barbershop outfits, some even with false moustaches. My role for the evening was as 'Uncle Sam'. A number of weeks before the event I had written to Jimmy Cagney telling him about this promotion and enclosed a 10 inch by 8 inch photograph of myself as 'Uncle Sam'. Jimmy kindly signed this and returned it to me, along with a photograph of himself and a record of the songs from the soundtrack of his film *Yankee Doodle Dandy*. My eleven year old son Christopher came as Huckleberry Finn, and Chico dressed up as Calamity Jane.

Irish Night. Arthur as Bing Crosby and the Jackson Dancers.

Mrs Kennedy, who owned several record shops in Leeds, gave us a hundred copies of the Doris Day hit single *My Secret Love* which were used as additional prizes on special USA flyer games.

Many members loved the Bing Crosby numbers that were played from time to time so we held a Bing Crosby night. We had a member who played the accordion very well, and Bing numbers were a favourite of his. Enquiries were also made if any gentlemen could sing like Crosby. We needed another focus for the entertainment however and the accordion sound eventually suggested a link. Bing's grandparents had come from Ireland so what could be nicer than Irish dancers. The Jackson Dancers, who were all young girls, were booked to appear. Their outfits were all made by their parents. The youngest dancer was only four years old.

The stage had been dressed with some old linen sheets draped to look like mountain rocks and branches from some trees on our car park had been brought in, to suggest a rural backdrop. Four members came up on stage to sing songs in the Bing Crosby manner, and were well received by a full house. Everyone was delighted by the fine Irish dancing from the Jackson Dancers. It was only three weeks to Christmas, so I donned a sweater and a golf trilby and, at the back of the dancers, I sang *You're All I Want for Christmas*. It went down well. I had never done an impression of Bing on stage before but nevertheless felt we had not let him down. There were a couple of special games with good money prizes so everyone went home happy.

The *Dominion* was still my main job of course, and planning the forthcoming attractions for the patrons was still a pleasure. We had a run of these one year: Easter Parades, Easter Bonnets and an outstanding Shrove Tuesday where all the female staff wore a waitress uniform from Jacomelli's, one of the city centre restaurants. Curry's electrical shop loaned four mobile electric grills which were mounted on the stage. A full catering size pack of pancake mixture was supplied by Readman's of Leeds Market.

Four game winners were brought to the front as contestants to make as many pancakes as they could in fifteen minutes! The winner of this contest was chosen by one of the directors of Jacomelli's, Mr Julio Vesparano. The prize for the winner was a free meal for two at Jacomelli's. Prior to the contest Mr Vesparano had himself made pancakes for all the management and myself.

Cue 14–ENTRANCE WITH DUSTBINS

ANOTHER DIVERSION FROM activities at the *Dominion* came one day with a telephone call to home and a deep male voice said, 'I know a lot about you. Would you care to come down next Monday at 10.30am?' This would be Bank Holiday Monday in 1986 and Radio Leeds wanted me to chat about my life in cinema, on stage and at Mecca.

I arrived at the studios in Woodhouse Lane by taxi at 9.45am and went to the main doors, but they appeared to be locked and there was no light visible anywhere. I was beginning to suspect that this was all a prank, but looked around and found two rather smelly dustbins at the side of a partially opened door at the rear of the building. Sliding between these bins I pushed the door open and found myself in a corridor. What an entrance for a BBC chat show! Suddenly a door opened and a bearded man of about thirty asked, 'Who are you?'.

I replied, 'I'm Artie Riley. I think I'm here to chat on the radio.'

'Yes' replied the man, 'and I think I forgot to go to the main door to let you in. My name is Alvin Kaye. I'm the Producer,' and laughing, he showed me into the studio. As it was Bank Holiday Monday he was running the whole show alone.

Alvin Kaye in his usual zany mood.

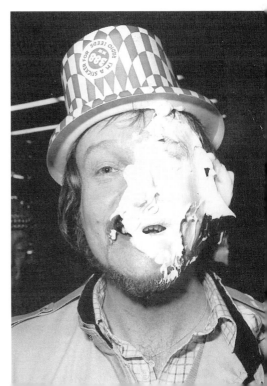

When we got into the studio Alvin took charge, controlling the sound, setting the introduction to the programme, and finally introducing me. We had a great time with lots of laughs on the show. There was quite a response from the listeners about the early cinemas I mentioned and there were a number of requests that I return to continue to talk more in this vein. A deal was signed between myself and Radio Leeds for me to present a programme entitled *Films on Friday*. If Friday was my day off from the *Dominion* then I went out 'live', but if not it was recorded. We made ninety-eight programmes in all.

There have been many times when Radio Leeds have called on me during the period when the studios were at the Merrion Centre in Leeds. One occasion was an *In Town Tonight* programme with Rory O'Dowd, a presenter with a wonderful voice. We worked together on a Monte Rey tribute, as well as one for Gracie Fields. Another featured the trio Los Paraguayos, with their leader Alberto Parana. A special programme for me was when Dame Anna Neagle allowed me to take part in her Radio Leeds programme; after all I was the fifteen year old kid who fell down the stairs at the *Paramount* and injured his neck whilst carrying her film *Sixty Glorious Years*. She had visited the *Paramount* that same morning for a private viewing of the film.

For me personally, the radio programme brought a new life. I researched, compiled and presented it. I also used my own records, sound tracks and letters. All this took hours to complete and for an introduction to the programme, the Twentieth Century Fox fanfare was used. Alvin's introduction each week varied from, 'He's only here for the money. Young Arthur Riley,' or 'He's here: no clothes on, but his spectacles are lovely,' or the one I preferred as it was the original, 'He's the fella that broke into Radio Leeds via two dustbins; Our Arthur.'

I felt that I had made it to the BBC for a long time to come. All was going well with the radio programme, and I was receiving between one and two hundred letters a month asking a variety of

In the studio for *Films on Friday*.

In the foyer of Radio Leeds.

questions, some easy, some more awkward. The research was tiring, but it was worth the effort to keep the programme up to the standard I liked. I sometimes got the odd letter to the effect that I was making it all up, but I could always back up what I was talking about because of my collection of scrapbooks, letters and photographs.

One very pleasant encounter I had there, was with Topol, the great star of *Fiddler on the Roof*. Years before, when he was appearing in this show in London, I had written to him requesting, as usual, a signed photograph. Now Topol does not send out photographs, he writes you a charming letter, signs it and then does a self-portrait of himself and the poor Jew Tevye. He was coming out of the studio at Radio Leeds after doing an interview just as I was going in to do *Films on Friday*. I introduced myself and thanked him for his unusual response. What a voice he has. He asked me many questions about my programme, but despite my best efforts, was not able to modify his schedule to appear on my show.

Cue 15–**UNICEF**

BEFORE WORKING FOR MECCA I had managed the record department of Vallance's in the Headrow, Leeds, which was a hectic position, and where there was little time for promotions after displaying and selling the records. Although not a promotion as such, we did have a visit in the department from Tiny Tim, who was appearing at the Batley Variety Club that week. He was, of course, received in a most courteous way by myself and my staff, but really and truly, he was the most untidily dressed celebrity I had ever met.

Around 1970 David Vallance, Wyn Calvin the Welsh comedian, Jane Terry and myself were invited to a 'Mead and Cheese' morning at the home of Doreen Sumners, a well-know television and radio personality. This charming lady was hosting the event to raise funds for UNICEF. One of the guests was Mannie Cussins, who was a prominent business man in and around Leeds, and on the board of Leeds United Football Club. After Wyn, Jane and myself had done our party pieces to support this special charity a discussion was held about UNICEF, and at the end I found that I had been voted chairman of the Leeds Branch of UNICEF. This meant a hard-working year ahead. Meetings were held in a large room at Peters Furnishing store, which was owned by Mr Cussins.

As part of my duties for UNICEF I had to arrange a promotion to tie in with the film *Song of Norway* which was being shown at the *Odeon* in the Merrion Centre (a beautiful cinema, but sadly now closed). I approached the *Odeon* who put on a special screening of the film for us; all the proceeds went to UNICEF. The Norwegian government sent traditional costumes as worn by their people, along with garlands and their national flag. The staff from Vallance's record department were invited to the special showing and they wore the Norwegian costumes. Among the young stars at that time was David, or Dai as he like to be called, Bradley, who was a star of the film *Kes* and, with Philip Maskery, the Yorkshire TV producer of *The Flaxton Boys*. Both David and Philip attended the screening as did Wyn Calvin and Jane Terry. Harry Secombe, who had a part in the film also came along for an hour. This was the number one local venture for UNICEF during my time as chairman and I am glad to say it was a success, though quite a headache to organise and control.

Late in 1970 I was invited to London to attend a UNICEF gala

The charity screening of *The Song of Norway* in aid of UNICEF, at the *Odeon*, Merrion Centre. The stars in attendance (left to right), David 'Dai' Bradley, Philip Maskery, Arthur and Wyn Calvin at the tombola.

and meeting. The trip commenced at Leeds City Station and I took with me a mobile recording machine which enabled me to record a commentary on the journey together with my thoughts and impressions of London. It was great fun, especially at Covent Garden where the market workers were preparing their stalls. This was before the actual fruit and vegetable market was moved to another area and the whole area re-furbished. I was mingling with the people working in the market and who made it the unique place that it was. I was dressed that day in a lounge suit and wore a bow tie rather than a conventional tie which caused a number of rather pointed remarks.

One, an old fashioned Cockney said, 'Cor Blimey! Are you coming dancing mate? Ya looks loveley!'

I took to the humour straight away and began taping everything.

Those whom I recorded were interested in what I was doing in London and I told them of UNICEF and it problems. They were full of support for the charity and as I made my way out, the first bloke who had asked me if I was going dancing shouted, 'Here y'are guv; the lads have collected for the kids!' and he handed me a large sealed envelope full of money!

Like a roving reporter I asked many of the people of all types and nationalities that I met that day about UNICEF and explained that they were being recorded for a big UNICEF meeting that was being held in London. One chap I came across was a street newspaper seller. He was disabled, having lost both his legs, and operated from a makeshift wheelchair. His name was C A Atkins and we chatted away whilst I recorded the conversation. He explained that he was happy selling newspapers and that this outdoor pitch was his in all weathers, summer and winter. I asked how he managed to keep warm in winter and his reply was, 'I drinks antifreeze Guv'nor.' A genuine cockney and a brave man.

Eventually I arrived at Rediffusion TV studios, where I met the late Eamonn Andrews. He was very kind and spoke on my tape about *This Is Your Life*, and wished us all the best. I made my way finally to the large hall where the UNICEF gala and meeting was being held, but was not allowed to take the tape recorder or camera into the room itself. We soon found out why. Danny Kaye, the chief fund raiser for UNICEF at that time, was appearing, along with Dustin Hoffman and Faye Dunaway. Each branch chairman was congratulated on their promotion of the charity and for their fund raising efforts. The final item was Danny Kaye and his daughter singing the UNICEF song; they had put words to the French tune *Abba Dabba Hoof Pop Pop*. Faye Dunaway and Dustin Hoffman later gave me a fifteen minute interview on tape.

*Cue 16–*Beside the Seaside

IN AUGUST 1976 MY WIFE CHICO and I decided to take two of the boys, Jeff and Chris, on a much needed holiday. The boys were working hard at school, and Chico always worked hard looking after our home and preparing meals, so it would be nice for her to have someone else making the meals for a change. Jeff had just finished a full week at Cross Green School starring in the title role of *Oliver*; like his Dad, he tried the Boards.

We had chosen a nice hotel at Morecambe and the mid August weather was terrific. One day we went to the beach, equipped with a picnic. The boys and I were in swimming trunks; Chico preferred a summer dress. Chris, who was nine years old at the time, wanted to go down to the sea. I could not swim due to having perforated eardrums from an accident when I was much younger, but Chris could, and he was good at it. He ran down to the sea with me keeping a close watch. Fortunately I have good eyesight and I suddenly noticed that, a few yards out to sea, two people appeared to be in trouble, with a good risk of drowning if something was not done quickly. I pointed them out to Chris who said immediately, 'I'll swim out to them Dad'.

This was an awkward situation for me as a non-swimmer. Chris and I waded into the sea together; I had to stop when the sea came up to my neck but Chris carried on and swam up to them. I saw him grab first one and then the other and he began to push them towards me. They were both unconcious. I grabbed hold of the first person, a lady, and dragged her through the sea to the sands; Chris managed to pull the man alongside. There was nobody else around, but fortunately the tide was going out, so I told Chris to run along the beach to where the tractor, that gave summer visitors trailer rides along the beach, was parked, and ask the driver to come to us. Chris then had to get someone to call an ambulance while I tried hard to attend to the couple. I tried every way I could to revive them; keeping them together for warmth. Their bodies were all sorts of funny colours, then all at once the girl started to vomit and a couple of seconds later the man too was sick. They continued to move a little which I hoped was a good sign. The tractor, with Chris on it, was now moving fast in our direction. The driver and I lifted the couple on to the trailer; they were still being sick and floundering as we raced back along the beach to the waiting ambulance. We left the scene and returned to Chico and Jeff, where we enjoyed the picnic. Chico said, 'Oh, you missed the ambulance and police. Something must have gone wrong.' Chris then told her what had happened. Chico gave us both a terrific kiss. She knew I could not swim and saw that I might have been in danger too.

An ice-cream van had arrived on the beach by now and naturally we all wanted one. Now, I was always a great fan of Max Wall and as I was being served and passing the ice-creams to the boys I kept saying, 'Thank yew' in my best Max Wall style.

The ice-cream man said, 'Hey, that's a good Max Wall sound. Do you do the boards?' I replied that I was an ex-pro and he replied, 'I've an agency in the town. Don't suppose you could do a spot Saturday and Sunday night at the *Station Hotel* in the city centre? I'd pay £160 for the two spots.'

As it meant extra money to spend on our holiday I readily accepted. All went well at the *Station Hotel* and we all enjoyed the extra and unexpected spending money.

Arriving back from holiday meant returning to the go-go-go of life at the Mecca and we soon forgot all about the incident on the beach. At the end of August however, I received a letter postmarked Morecambe. It was from a resident there and she had been on the beach when Chris and I walked away after rescuing the drowning couple. She had also been in the audience of one of the shows that I had done at the *Station Hotel* and she had recognised me as one of the people involved in the beach incident and had written to say that the Morecambe police wanted to see me. They came over to interview Chris and myself about the rescue. In due course the *Yorkshire Evening Post* arrived to take a photograph of Chris and myself receiving a bravery Diploma from the police. I felt very proud of Chris because at nine years old it was he who had swum out and was able to grab those two drowning people. Little did we know then, but Chris later joined the Royal Navy!

Cue 17–**JUNIORS**

OUR SON JEFFREY HAD BEEN AN apprentice lighting engineer at the *Grand Theatre*, Leeds with Mr Kaye (Mr Rosa) and ultimately, when he had completed his apprenticeship, a circle box was converted so that he could have the latest Hi-tech equipment panel, to electronically change and set what ever lighting was required for the shows. Jeff was known by many of the television and theatre stars such as Roy Hudd, Bernard Miles, Christopher Gable of Northern Ballet and Mike Harding. The people at BBC Television in Leeds also used his talents on a number of occasions. He received a letter from the ballerina Dame Margot Fonteyn who thanked him for his lighting skills that enhanced her dancing.

In due course he was ready to move on to bigger challenges; Chico and I saw the last show he lit at the *Grand*. It was the new London production of *Oklahoma*. During this period he had arranged to take me to the *Grand* to see the Pasadena Roof Orchestra, who were appearing there. Just before the show started 'Mr Rosa' came looking for us; one of the men who was employed on the 'limes' had not turned in. Could we step in? We did and greatly enjoyed ourselves.

Jeff had been selected by Leeds City Council to take on a new venture. The Council had bought the old synagogue at the bottom of Chapeltown Road, taken out all the seats and made a shell of a theatre. The Council asked Jeff to transform the building into a fine dance theatre. Which is just what he did. He set up the stage, rigging it for computer controlled lighting and much more. It was soon ready and in moved the Dance School of Leeds which became the Northern School of Contemporary Dance, with its head administrator Nadine Senior MBE. The School of Dance visited many parts of the UK, and was universally well received. They also began to attend dance festivals around the world. Many favourable impressions were made on potential students and heads of departments within the schools and colleges as a result of their attendances at these festivals. Jeff became a lecturer at the school and travelled with them when on tour. His particular interest was the lighting, which he oversaw personally.

The Northern School of Contemporary Dance, along with many other schools attended a festival of dance in Japan in July 1993. My family and I, like many other people, knew, that the Japanese word

In memory of Jeff the Northern School of Contemporary Dance renamed its theatre the *Riley Theatre*.

for goodbye is *Sayonara*, but little did we know how much it would mean to us. Jeff suffered a brain haemorrhage whilst in Japan and was on a life support machine for three days in the main hospital in Kobe. The Northern School arranged for Jeff's wife Carolyn and his brother Christopher to fly out to be with him, but Jeff tragically died there on the 31 July aged thirty-three. The Northern School arranged for Jeff's body to be brought home for burial. He left a wife, Carolyn and two children, Martin Andrew and Laura Marie. There were

Just For Jeff

The Dome Theatre,
Leeds *6.11.93*

Stephanie Ferguson

THIS wasn't a wake but a celebration of the life and work of Jeff Riley, technical director of the Northern School of Contemporary Dance, who died in July following a brain haemorrhage while at a student dance festival in Japan.

Friends and colleagues paid tribute to Jeff in words, dance and music at this benefit concert for his family. A perfectionist, no-nonsense teacher, brilliant Mr Fix-It, Jeff was the consummate technician whether lighting ballet for Dame Margot Fonteyn or working on the West Indian Carnival. He made The Dome one of the UK's leading dance venues and from January it will be known as The Riley Theatre in his memory.

Dancing sadly, but with great conviction, the students turned Philip Taylor's suitably named *Quiet Strength* into a powerful requiem. Like Sinatra, everyone did it their way in homage to Jeff. RJC Dance Theatre were red hot in their fresh and different fusion of reggae, soul and jazz with a sinuous solo from Donald Edwards and scorching duo from Edward Lynch and De Napoli Clarke.

Phoenix Dance Company added to the heat with the fast and flagrant *Fatal Strategy*, or edgy eroticism, pounding action and leopardskin bras. Jeff would have approved.

Looking uncannily like Fonteyn, ballet lecturer Elizabeth Rao danced her poignant tribute to classical guitar while Tanya Cusan sang in Spanish. Paul Clayden strutted ice cool with Namron in *Crocodile* with its bluesy riffs while Shirley Pickles and Malcolm Jacobs turned on the acrobatics in *Sweet Gypsy*.

There were tears and memories and wisecracks about the lighting. But as we left Tina Turner said it all. He was "simply the best."

A write up of the benefit concert for Jeff Riley.

numerous tributes to Jeff from people in radio and TV and many of the stars for whom he had designed and lit shows, sent their own tokens of appreciation. In memory of Jeff the Northern School of Contemporary Dance renamed its theatre the *Riley Theatre*.

Our youngest son, Christopher, joined the Royal Navy after a period in the Sea Cadets. He passed all of his courses with flying colours and took up his duties as sight and sound telegraphist which he enjoyed for a while, then he decided that he would like to be in submarines. He was told that he could not 'chop and change' like that. It was the Royal Navy not Riley's Navy. Christopher did not give up, but, after a lot of argument, gave up his navy career and is now a successful printer. He has settled down and has a wife and three children. The only 'cue' for Christopher is the one he uses at the snooker table!

Our eldest son, Howard, had decided to leave the motor trade, where he had worked since being apprenticed. So, by pulling a few strings, I was able to arrange for him to take up employment with Mecca as assistant manager at Bradford. However, he did not find this to his liking.

The night the Northern School of Contempary Dance was renamed the *Riley Theatre*, in Jeff's memory. From left to right: Arthur, Howard, Jeff's widow Carolyn, Chico, Chris and his wife Beverly.

*Cue 18–*VE DAY 1985 AND OLD MOTHER RILEY

WE ARE ALL AWARE THAT SOME people do not wish to be reminded about the war in plays, films or literature, but in 1985 I had an idea that would commemorate the happy event of cessation of hostilities in Europe. The commemoration of this event would be acceptable to the older members, for after all, each one had made a contribution to the war effort in some way or another. So we put on a Victory in Europe celebration theme night on the fortieth anniversary of this. The members were asked for photographs of themselves in uniform or at work during the war, so that they could be displayed with a big sign asking, 'What did you do in the war, Mum/Dad?' We got our usual excellent response to this, and I proposed to Mecca that we should put on a meal. But it was to be a wartime meal, and those who could produce a old Ration Book could have an extra treat, a free thermos flask to put your tea or soup in for home.

Mecca agreed, so now we had to think of ways to attract additional members. There would be extra games, with extra prize money of course, but what else could we offer that had not been done before? Once again I drew on my old stage act and decided on portraying Robb Wilton as the fireman. Leeds City Fire Brigade loaned us a wartime uniform and fire trailer complete with pump and hoses.

So, leaning against this in Robb Wilton style, I started on a monologue that began, 'The day war broke out I joined the Leeds City Fire Brigade...' and followed it up with impressions of the wartime stars. We asked if any women members wanted to do a party piece; a number entered and the winner was a lady who had come dressed as a munitions worker in blue overalls and a headscarf. Her partner played the accordion and she sang wartime favourites for fifteen minutes! Leeds City Transport Department's vintage section kindly loaned a vintage double decker bus with driver and, during the interval, members were taken on a commemorative trip to Roundhay Park and back. The club had been decorated with red, white and blue bunting, with a large Union Jack flag over the circle front, and each member was given a Union Jack flag on a stick to wave at a given signal.

Another spot that was well received by everyone was when we played a tape that began with the voice of Victor Sylvester

The outside of the *Dominion* decorated for the VE day promotion in 1985.

announcing 'Slow, slow, quick, quick, slow' and leading into a medley of dance tunes. People were dancing in the aisles and in the coffee bar area; nobody had forgotten the lovely tempo of this orchestra. The members enjoyed it so much that they asked for a replay!

I had also wondered what well-known radio, TV or recording star could be invited. Fortunately a dear pal from my Music Hall days, Ronnie Hilton, was 'resting'.

When I approached Ronnie Hilton about appearing, his response was:

> *If you display a big photograph of me as Lance Corporal R Hill (his real name) of the Highland Light Infantry, then I will come for nowt and do three songs with a wartime sing-a-long for everyone.*

He also said he would bring his own accompanist. The photograph duly arrived and was displayed in the main foyer with a tartan background and a banner proclaiming: 'Our wartime star is coming along too - Ronnie Hilton'

With all this in mind I rang Yorkshire Television *Calendar* programme and they promised to attend. Everyone was delighted, especially Ronnie, and in his blunt way he told me: 'That is bloody good Arthur; bloody good publicity for us all, including me.'

My wife had suggested that we display on the top of the canopy outside, red, white and blue bunting, and VE in eight inch high letters, together with a cut-out of a sailor so that all who passed the *Dominion* were in not doubt about what we were celebrating.

On the whole, everything went to plan, but as time was going on there was no sign of the camera crew from Yorkshire Television; everyone was beginning to think that I had been having them on. The manager was furious and Ronnie Hilton said, 'It is a bloody bad publicity stunt,' and I was nearly frantic. Just as I was about to throw in the towel the camera crew arrived and began to set up. Then Ronnie turned to me and said, 'I've sent my accompanist home, thinking you'd let me down.'

We quickly went back stage to my office. One of the songs he had been due to sing was, *I'll be with you in apple blossom time*, which I had on record. I put it on the turntable, as Ronnie was worried about whether it was in the right key or not. After making sure the sound was not audible to the audience, we played it through. Fortunately it was in Ronnie's key. As the TV crew were still setting up, Ronnie asked the television floor manager for a run-through. He went centre stage, I turned up the volume on the record player and Yorkshire

Television went to town. It went extremely well and was on the *Calendar* programme that night.

The record was actually one by the Black and White Minstrels, and Ronnie remarked ironically, 'If we get found out we'll both get our Equity cards withdrawn!' Still, the show must go on. It was considered to be a very good day with over 1,000 members attending; we all received a good bonus. There was only one problem after the event though – what to do with all the bunting. The manager was only too glad for it to go to some person or organisation that could use it, so my friend Shirley Haines was the grateful recipient for the church garden party. We received a very nice letter from the vicar thanking us.

The character of Old Mother Riley was such a well known one, through Music Hall and film that it seems odd, given the coincidence of the names, that I had never attempted to do an impression of her. One of my final promotions for Mecca rectified this. We had to have a plot that would please the members, and, as there was such a big stage at the *Dominion*, it meant that we were able to set it out as Mother Riley's home. We had to have authenticity for the set, so we knocked together an old-looking table and Welsh dresser with pots and plates on every shelf. Not wanting to smash up perfectly good new plates we appealed to members for old and cracked crockery, while not letting them into the secret. They may have thought I was going crazy, but the crockery soon began to pile up.

I would take the part of Mother Riley dressed in rags, shawl and bonnet, but who would play the role of my daughter Kitty? Despite all her arguments to the contrary about being too shy to appear on stage I eventually managed to persuade my wife Chico to do it. After that my attention turned to the pantomime cow! Our manager, Jimmy Jackson, volunteered to be the front half of the cow, but who could we get to be the back half? We both thought that our assistant manager, would be perfect and Jimmy said he would make sure that he would comply.

Around this time Kerry Gold butter was making its mark and it was incorporated into the story, which was that Mother Riley suggests to Kitty that because they are so hard up, they ought to sell the cow. After much bickering Kitty agrees, but before they sell her they need a bucketful of milk. I contacted the makers of Kerry Gold and after outlining the story and the reason for the promotion to them, told them that we needed butter to make the final punchline work. They agreed to deliver the butter along with a new line they were introducing into England, Kerry Silver.

To open the 'panto', Mother Riley would be waiting at home for the return of her daughter Kitty. It would run through the usual patter, 'Where's my daughter? I don't know if it is home time, supper time or closing time. Who is she with? What do they call him? Where's he live? I'll show her how her late father died!' and so on. We held some rehearsals for the show and then announced it to the customers, along with the chance to win Kerry Gold and Kerry Silver butter on a special 'Irish Flutter' game along with added prize money.

On the day itself we had a sell-out, with again over a 1,000 members vying for their favourite seats. The opening had Mother Riley walking on stage with a shopping trolley saying, 'Sorry I'm late, but I've just been shop lifting. You can tell because I've got my running shoes on.' Then sitting down she launched into a diatribe. This was the cue for Kitty to enter saying she was sorry she was late. 'Sit down darling Kitty. Would you like some egg broth?' she is asked.

Of course she would, so Mother Riley got six eggs out of the pan

Arthur and Chico in the Old Mother Riley sketch.

The Old Mother Riley cast, (left to right) Chico, David Denton, Jimmy Jackson and Arthur.

which was on a small cooking unit, and served the water they had been standing in as egg broth. The teapot had been doctored with a broken handle stuck back on with Sellotape so that when Kitty lifted it up to pour a cup of tea the handle and the pot parted company. This was the cue to start an argument that deteriorated into a 'real set to', where Mother Riley and Kitty throw and smash the already broken crockery. Members were also invited, 'If you want to join in the row, come and help smash my happy home to bits.' They did and had a lovely time.

In the aftermath of the row Mother Riley and Kitty are upset and Mother Riley mourns for the destruction of the home and the crockery. Finally agreeing that Rosie the cow will have to be sold to pay for it all, Kitty insists that a final bucket of milk be drawn from her before she goes. Kitty brings on the cow and in true 'panto' style set up the, 'Will we have to sell the cow?' 'Oh yes we will,' 'Oh no we wont,' routine with full audience participation. Kitty then milked the cow for the last time, and as she did so a few pounds of Kerry butter dropped into the bucket.

Kitty shouted 'Mother, Mother, Rosie's not giving any milk,' and Mother Riley exclaimed: 'Ha. She's not got any milk left?' at which Kitty brought the bucket of butter to me. Mother Riley gasped and shouted to the audience, 'We won't have to sell Rosie now. We can sell the Kerry Gold and Kerry Silver butter and live off the profits!' at which Kitty caressed Rosie. The manager emerged from the front end of Rosie, to loud applause and cheering.

'But wait ladies and gentlemen,' I shouted, 'I told you I would get him in 'the end!' and the assistant manager, emerged to tumultuous applause.

It was a great end to a grand time ...

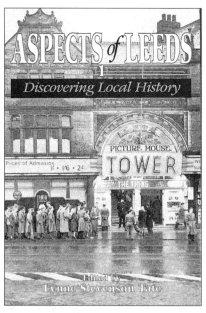

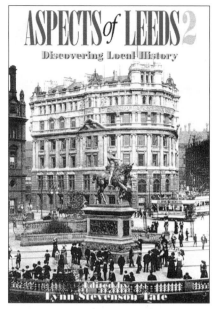

ASPECTS OF LEEDS 1
Discovering Local History
Edited by Lynne Stevenson Tate

ASPECTS LEEDS 2
Discovering Local History
Edited by Lynne Stevenson Tate

ISBN: 1-871647-38-X – £9.95

ISBN: 1-871647-59-2 – £9.95